A TEMPLAR BOOK

First published in the UK in 2024 by Templar Books,
an imprint of Bonnier Books UK
4th Floor, Victoria House,
Bloomsbury Square, London, WC1B 4DA
Owned by Bonnier Books
Sveavägen 56, Stockholm, Sweden
www.bonnierbooks.co.uk

Text copyright © 2024 by Mike Barfield
Illustration copyright © 2024 by Franziska Höllbacher
Design copyright © 2024 by Templar Books

10 9 8 7 6 5 4 3 2 1

All rights reserved

ISBN 978-1-80078-372-0

This book was typeset in Providence Sans,
Bokka, Chubby Chap, Mind Boggle, Boucherie,
Fruity Snack.
The illustrations were created digitally.
Edited by Sophie Hallam
Fact-checked by Houda Hasbini
Designed by Anna Ring
Production by Neil Randles

Printed in China

✯ ✯ ✯
For Anne, who invented me a whole new career — M.B.
✯ ✯ ✯

✯ ✯ ✯
To Julian, with whom I share a home – and my love for cats. — F.H.
✯ ✯ ✯

CONTENTS

1 HIGH AND MIGHTY ... 9
ROLLERCOASTER ... 10
SKYSCRAPER ... 12
DIÉBÉDO FRANCIS KÉRÉ ... 14
SUPERMARKET ... 16
WIND TURBINE ... 18
NO PLACE LIKE HOME! ... 20

FEATURING DIÉBÉDO FRANCIS KÉRÉ ON PAGE 14

2 GOING PLACES ... 21
BICYCLE ... 22
BULLET TRAIN ... 24
ELECTRIC VEHICLE ... 26
BERTHA BENZ ... 28
DRONE ... 30
JUST THE TICKET! ... 32

FEATURING BERTHA BENZ ON PAGE 28

3 HOUSE AND HOME ... 33
FLUSH TOILET ... 34
PERCY SPENCER ... 36
BUBBLE WRAP ... 38
DOMESTIC DOG ... 40
GREAT MISTAKES ... 42

FEATURING PERCY SPENCER ON PAGE 36

4 FOOD AND DRINK ... 43
HAMBURGER ... 44
FIZZY DRINKS ... 46
MOMOFUKU ANDO ... 48
POTATO CHIPS ... 50
FOOD FOR THOUGHT ... 52

FEATURING MOMOFUKU ANDO ON PAGE 48

5 WEAR AND TEAR 53
    DENIM JEANS 54
    SPORTS SHOE 56
    PATSY O'CONNELL SHERMAN 58
    SCHOOL RULES! 60

FEATURING PATSY O'CONNELL SHERMAN ON PAGE 58

6 FUN AND GAMES 61
    SKATEBOARD 62
    TEDDY BEAR 64
    LONNIE JOHNSON 66
    TOY BALLOON 68
    PLANET MIRTH! 70

FEATURING LONNIE JOHNSON ON PAGE 66

7 RUN AND JUMP 71
    FOOTBALL 72
    TABLE TENNIS 74
    KANŌ JIGORŌ 76
    JOLLY GOOD SPORTS! 78

FEATURING KANŌ JIGORŌ ON PAGE 76

8 SCREEN AND HEARD 79
    VIDEO GAMES 80
    TABLET COMPUTER 82
    JAWED KARIM 84
    SMARTPHONE 86
    BRAVE NEW WORLD 88
    YOUNG WIZARDS 90
    PATENT'S PROGRESS 92

FEATURING JAWED KARIM ON PAGE 84
UTUBE

CHAPTER 1
HIGH AND MIGHTY

The world is bursting with buildings, and no wonder with a population of about eight billion people! In this chapter, we reveal a selection of striking structures that are record-makers and record-breakers, as well as some that are just plain fun! First, let's build the excitement with four fantastic facts:

WORLD'S OLDEST HOME

Knap of Howar in the Orkney Islands, Scotland, is over **5,000 years old**! It lacks a roof but still has a lovely view of the sea.

WORLD'S HIGHEST SANDCASTLE — 21 m

Built in a sculpture park in Denmark in 2021, this pile of sand stood at just over 21 metres tall, helped by a small amount of **glue** and **clay** mixed in.

CHEATING?

BIGGEST BIRD-SHAPED BUILDING

Ashgabat International Airport in Turkmenistan, Asia, is built in the form of a giant **white falcon** swooping low.

FIRST BUILD ON MINECRAFT

Just 49 minutes after the computer game Minecraft launched in 2009, a player called 'Muku' built a **nine-block bridge**. Now over 170 million people play it each month!

9

SKYSCRAPER

HIGHLY INVENTIVE

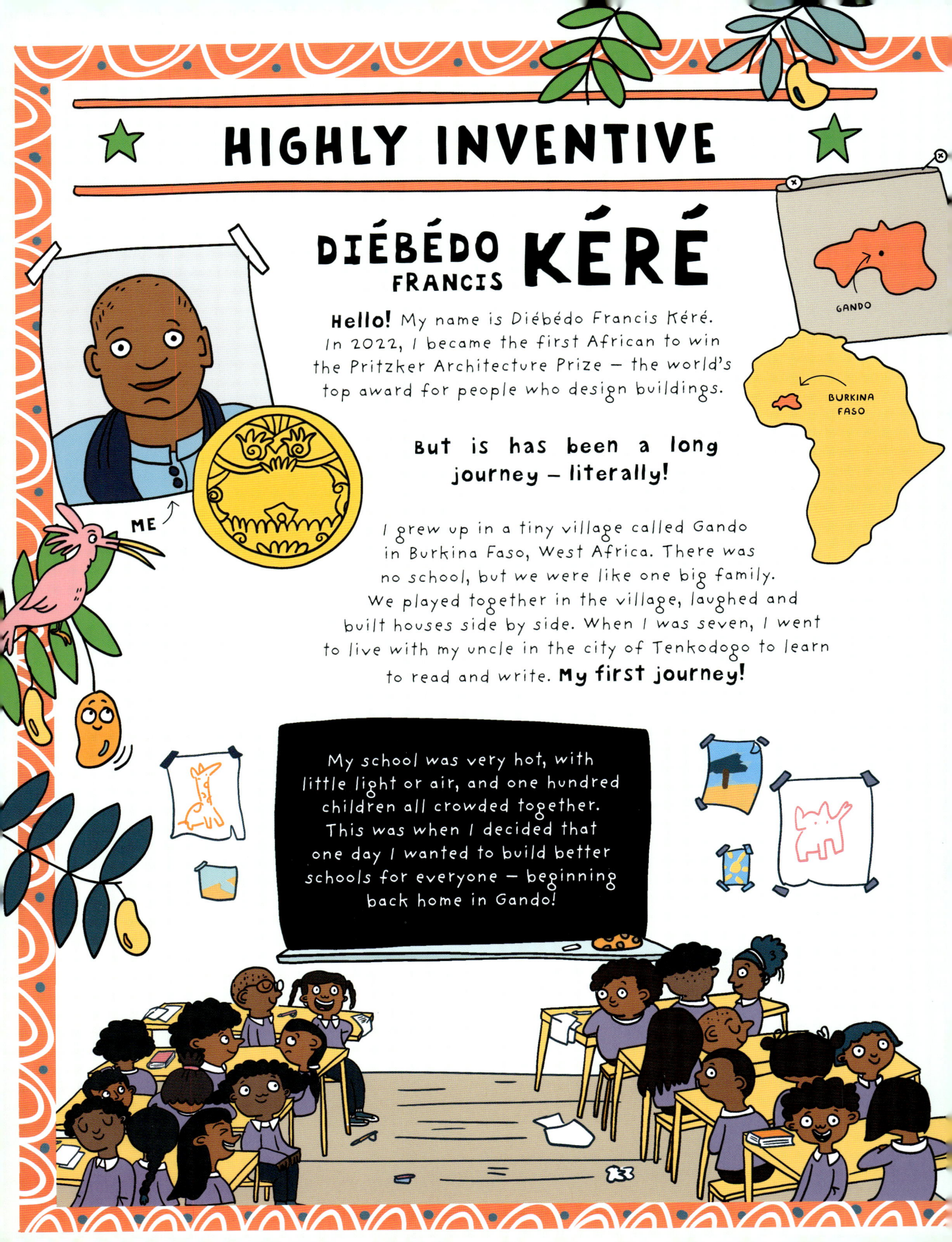

DIÉBÉDO FRANCIS KÉRÉ

← ME

GANDO

BURKINA FASO

Hello! My name is Diébédo Francis Kéré. In 2022, I became the first African to win the Pritzker Architecture Prize — the world's top award for people who design buildings.

But is has been a long journey — literally!

I grew up in a tiny village called Gando in Burkina Faso, West Africa. There was no school, but we were like one big family. We played together in the village, laughed and built houses side by side. When I was seven, I went to live with my uncle in the city of Tenkodogo to learn to read and write. **My first journey!**

My school was very hot, with little light or air, and one hundred children all crowded together. This was when I decided that one day I wanted to build better schools for everyone — beginning back home in Gando!

After leaving school, I became a carpenter, working with wood. Skills like these can take you far. Mine took me to Berlin, Germany, where I eventually went to college to study architecture.

Could I make my dream come true?

Maybe! I headed home to Gando to build an eco-friendly school with the help of the community. We made mud bricks rather than use expensive cement and planted mango trees for shade — as well as their tasty fruit!

It was finished in 2001 with a raised roof to beat the heat. I qualified as an architect soon afterwards and went back to build a high school, as well as homes for teachers too!

But, best of all, my cool school inspired others like it to be built. Now I have designed buildings all over the world that work with nature, not against it.

BENIN NATIONAL ASSEMBLY, PORTO-NOVO, BENIN

TUM TOWER, UNIVERSITY OF MUNICH, GERMANY

SERPENTINE PAVILION, LONDON, UK

It's been a great journey — and it isn't over yet!

15

SUPERMARKET

WHATEVER NEXT? CHECK IT OUT

NAME GAME

The word 'mall' comes from 'Pall Mall', a smart London street. However, 400 years ago it was a large field where rich people played a popular ball game. Buckingham Palace now stands nearby.

THE GREAT INDOORS

The world's first shopping mall was the Southdale Center in Edina, Minnesota, USA. Opened in 1956, architect Victor Gruen wanted to create a European-style high street indoors, free from cars.

MIGHTY MALL

The world's most massive mall is Iran Mall in the Iranian capital of Tehran. It has shops on seven floors covering an area greater than 270 football pitches!

HOT STUFF!

Volcano Buono Mall near Naples, Italy, is inside a giant grass-covered mound shaped like a shallow volcano. Its name means 'Good volcano', unlike nearby Mount Vesuvius, a real volcano that once destroyed the Roman city of Pompeii and all its shops and stalls.

17

WIND TURBINE

Hi! I'm a gust of wind heading for the world's tallest turbine.

SEE YOU IN A SHORT WHILE!

WHEEE!

MEANWHILE

Hi! That top turbine is me! 260 metres high and stood by the sea in Rotterdam, the Netherlands!

Few of you humans have seen me close-up because I'm so tall and big – each of my blades is the length of a football pitch.

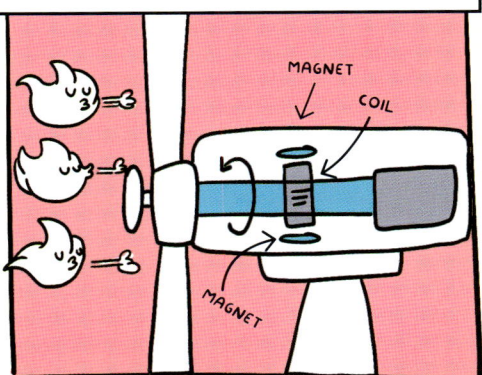

Wind hitting my blades pushes them round and turns a giant wire coil inside some powerful magnets...

MAGNET
COIL
MAGNET

...This generates electricity by an effect discovered in 1831 by British boffin Michael Faraday.

MEET ME AGAIN ON PAGE 68

A machine that turns motion into electricity is called a 'dynamo'.

YOU COULD SAY I HAVE A 'DYNAMIC PERSONALITY'!

Of course, humans have been working with wind for many centuries...

BOATS   WINDMILLS   KITES

But it took until 1887 for Scottish scientist James Blyth to build the world's first wind turbine.

SPIN!

WHY DIDN'T I THINK OF THIS SOONER?

IT'S A REAL LIGHTBULB MOMENT!

It lit the lamps in his holiday home!

Sadly, his idea was overlooked in favour of filthy fuels like coal being burnt in power stations.

WHAT A PITY... COUGH!

But a clean, green machine like me can power 16,000 homes without creating any greenhouse gases...

REMEMBER ME?

All thanks to gusts like this guy!

COMING THROUGH!

NOW I'M OFF TO FIND A SKYSCRAPER! BYE!

WORLD OF WONDERS

NO PLACE LIKE HOME!

Fancy spending a night inside an elephant, or turning your home into a toilet? Here are some of the oddest buildings in the world!

The **Upside-Down House** in Szymbark, Poland, is a top tourist attraction. You enter through a window in the roof!

The **Haines Shoe House** in Pennsylvania, USA, was built by a shoe salesman to advertise footwear. Wipe your feet before entering!

'**Lucy**' is a giant concrete elephant in New Jersey, USA, that doubles as a hotel. Don't forget to take a trunk!

This home in Miziara, Lebanon, is a full-sized replica of an **Airbus A380**, the world's largest passenger plane. Do you think the idea will take off?

A house in Oxford, England, has a giant fibreglass **shark** wedged in its roof!

The '**Toilet House**' in Suwon, South Korea, is now a museum all about toilets and has a giant, golden sculpture of a poo outside. Make sure you wash your hands!

CHAPTER 2
GOING PLACES

Humans have been on the move for the past 200,000 years: first on foot, then by water, horses, wheels and wings. In this chapter, we have the stories behind some of the cleanest, greenest ways to travel, and much more. So, get a move on! Let's start with some 'safety first' facts!

WORLD'S FIRST SPEED LIMIT

Introduced in Britain in 1865, motor car drivers had to keep below **1.6 km/h** in towns and have someone walk slowly in front with a red flag!

FIRST CHILD SAFETY SEAT

The modern-style car **safety seat** was invented in 1962 by Jean 'Jerry' Ames, a working British mum who wanted to keep her young son safe.

MOST CRASHED DRIVER

The crash test dummy known as **'Hybrid III'** was introduced in 1976.

Used by car makers across the world, if 'H III' could stand up he would be 1.75 metres tall.

ODDEST SAFETY MEASURE

It may sound scary, but most modern cars contain **high explosives**!

They are detonated by collisions to produce the nitrogen gas that inflates airbags.

CRASH!

21

BICYCLE

WHATEVER NEXT? PEDAL POWER!

ALIEN LIFE CYCLE

The world's best known bike is the BMX that flew across the moon in the 1982 blockbuster family film, E.T. the Extra-Terrestrial. The BMX that followed were out-of-this-world!

IS IT A BIRD?

BMX bikers can now compete in the Olympic Games. The sport involves tricks with names including the tailwhip, 'T-Bog', bunny hop and 'Superman', where the rider leaps with their arms held like a flying superhero.

SPEEDY SEB

Dutch athlete Sebastiaan Bowier hit a world record cycling speed of 133 km/h in 2013 by pedalling whilst lying down inside a giant, streamlined shell.

VERY HANDY!

Handcycles are three-wheeled bikes for people who use their arms to pedal. Amazingly, the earliest-known example dates back to 1655!

BULLET TRAIN

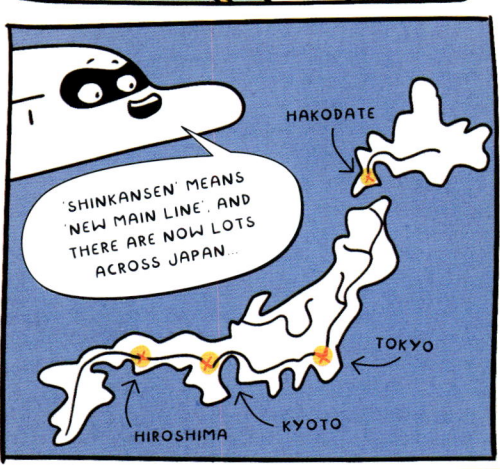

ELECTRIC VEHICLE

WHATEVER NEXT?
CURRENT AFFAIRS

PARKING SPACE
Tesla is the world's best-selling brand of EV. In 2018, Tesla owner Elon Musk fired his own electric sportscar into an endless orbit around the sun as a test for the space rockets he also makes.

FULL MOON
Fancy your own EV? There are three going spare on the moon! Nicknamed 'moon buggies', the Lunar Roving Vehicles were left behind by the USA's 'Apollo' missions of the early 1970s.

LOTTA BOTTLE
For most of the last century, the majority of the world's EVs were milk floats — slow-moving electric vans used for delivering bottled milk. Their quiet motors didn't disturb sleeping customers early in the morning. Shhh!

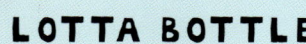

LIGHTNING FAST
The world's fastest electric vehicle is the Buckeye Bullet 3, built by students of Ohio State University. In 2016, it hit 495 km/h — about five times the local speed limit for cars!

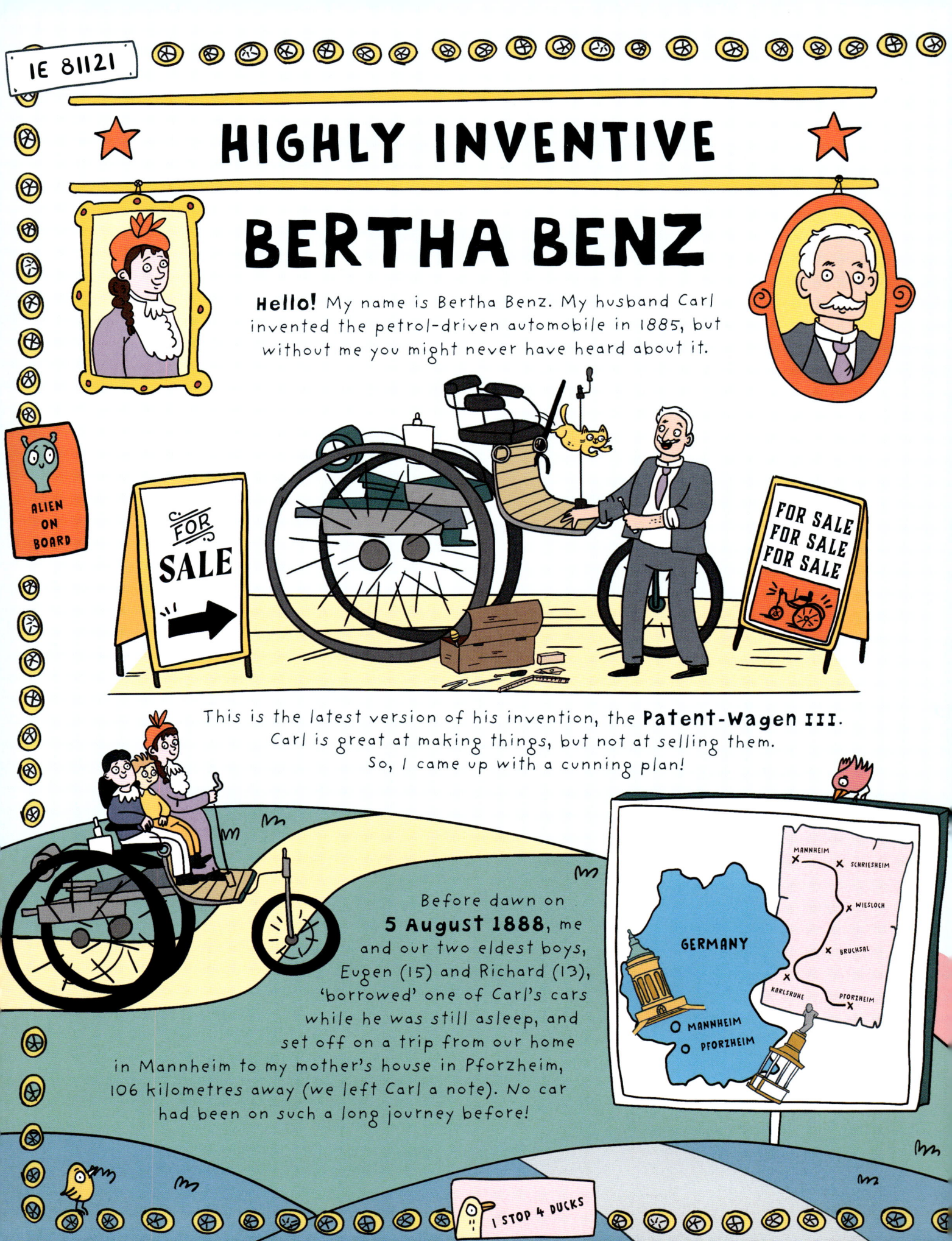

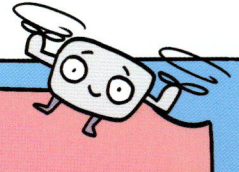

DRONE

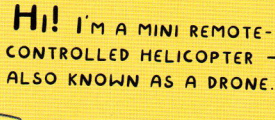

HI! I'M A MINI REMOTE-CONTROLLED HELICOPTER — ALSO KNOWN AS A DRONE.

WHIRR! WHIRR!

WHIRR! 'DRONE' SOUNDS DULL, BUT HELICOPTER HISTORY ISN'T!

IT GOES BACK TO ANCIENT CHINA AND SIMPLE FLYING TOYS WITH FEATHERS FOR ROTOR BLADES.

YOU SPIN IT BETWEEN YOUR HANDS?

YES! THEN IT FLIES TO THE SKIES!

ITALIAN EGGHEAD LEONARDO DA VINCI DESIGNED AN 'AERIAL SCREW' IN THE 1480s, BUT IT NEVER GOT OFF THE GROUND...

SIGH! WHAT ARE YOU SMILING AT?

THE NEXT FEW CENTURIES SAW MANY ATTEMPTS TO MAKE ROTOR-POWERED FLYING MACHINES WITHOUT SUCCESS. THEN, IN 1861, FRENCH INVENTOR GUSTAVE D'AMÉCOURT MADE A BREAKTHROUGH...

I INVENTED THE WORD 'HELICOPTER', FROM 'HELICO' MEANING 'SPIRAL' AND 'PTER' FROM THE GREEK FOR 'WING'.

helico + pter

IN 1907, ANOTHER FRENCH INVENTOR, LOUIS CHARLES BREGUET, FINALLY MADE THE FIRST MANNED HELICOPTER FLIGHT — JUST 60 CENTIMETRES ABOVE THE GROUND!

BUT IT STILL COUNTS. OUI?

HOVER! WOBBLE! 60CM

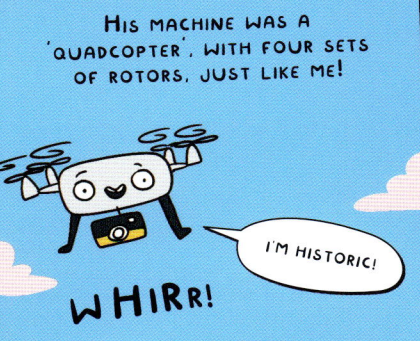

HIS MACHINE WAS A 'QUADCOPTER', WITH FOUR SETS OF ROTORS, JUST LIKE ME!

I'M HISTORIC!

WHIRR!

WHIRR!

AFTERWARDS, THE WORLD BUILT BIGGER AND BETTER HELICOPTERS.

TODAY, THE WORLD'S LARGEST HELICOPTER IS THE 40-METRE-LONG MIL MI-26. IT COULD LIFT THREE LARGE AFRICAN ELEPHANTS!

WHIRR!

NIFTY LITTLE BATTERY-POWERED DRONES CAME ALONG IN THE 1990s, AND NOW WE DO LOTS OF JOBS.

WHIRR!

MAPPING MOUNTAINS

WHIRR!

MAKING MOVIES

WHIRR! SQUIRT!

FIGHTING FIRES

WHIRR! HELP!

SAVING LIVES

WHIRR!

AS I SAID, DRONES AREN'T DULL! NOW, I'M OFF TO INSPECT A SKYSCRAPER. BYE!

WHATEVER NEXT?
GAME OF DRONES

SPACE AGE RACE

Drone racing is a sport where drones are steered at super-speed around special courses. Players wear virtual reality headsets and get to feel like they are sat in a tiny pilot's seat onboard!

THE DRONE DAILY

LIFE ON MARS

A small helicopter called 'Ingenuity' became the first object to fly on Mars in April 2021. It was sent by the US space agency NASA to help search for signs of life.

SPECIAL DELIVERY

In the future, goods, food and medicines may well be delivered to your home by drones. Several big businesses have made test flights but there are still safety concerns to overcome.

EYE IN THE SKY

Drones can be used to help with animal conservation by tracking endangered species and spotting poachers. However, elephants hate the noise they make, and can't see where it is coming from.

WORLD OF WONDERS

JUST THE TICKET!

How do you get to school in the mornings? Bus, bike or on foot? Here are some other ways the world gets to work!

Coco-taxis are popular in the Cuban capital Havana. Their name comes from being shaped like the large tropical nuts.

Brightly painted **'chicken buses'** run on the roads in Guatemala. Fancy a ride — or are you chicken?

The **bamboo trains** of Cambodia are motor-driven wooden platforms that travel on railway tracks. You sit on a simple mat!

Thailand's colourful **tuk-tuk taxis** take their name from the 'tuk-tuk-tuk' noise made by their motors.

On the island of Madeira, tourists can **toboggan** down the steep streets leading to the capital, Funchal.

The world's only surviving **hovercraft** service runs between the Isle of Wight and the UK mainland. You literally float on air!

CHAPTER 3
HOUSE AND HOME

The campfire was probably the first great household invention, back when caves were all the rage. Today, microwave ovens can heat food in a flash, but you don't get people or pets cosying up to them. In this chapter, we consider some common home comforts — including those for our furry, four-legged friends! But first, let's take a look at the huge variety of devices in our households — some are the stuff of science fiction!

MOST INFURIATED INVENTOR

In 1886, Josephine Cochrane of Illinois, USA, was driven to invent a **dishwasher** that spray-cleaned plates with water because she was sick of doing it.

MOST UNKNOWN INVENTOR

Fancy giving the carpets a quick **'spangler'**? The vacuum cleaner was actually invented in 1907 by James Spangler, who sold his idea to William Henry Hoover.

MOST GUARDED HOME

New York nurse Marie Van Brittan Brown invented the first **home security** system, with cameras inside and out, as she didn't enjoy coming home alone at night.

MOST INTRUSIVE INVENTION?

A **virtual assistant** constantly listens for commands while connected to the internet. In 2018, a parrot called Rocco used one to order a watermelon, ice cream and a kite.

33

FLUSH TOILET

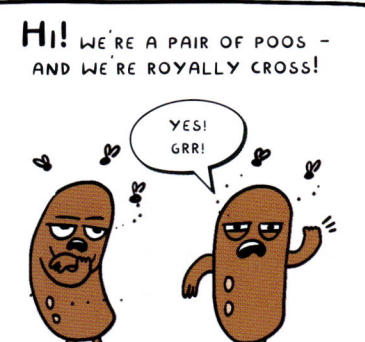

HI! WE'RE A PAIR OF POOS — AND WE'RE ROYALLY CROSS!

YES! GRR!

WE'RE CROSS WITH THIS ROYAL IN PARTICULAR...

GRR!

JUST OVER 400 YEARS AGO, ENGLISH QUEEN ELIZABETH I BECAME THE WORLD'S FIRST FAMOUS NAME TO USE A FLUSHING TOILET.

IT MAKES A CHANGE FROM YE THRONE...

THE FLUSH TOILET WAS INVENTED BY HER GODSON JOHN HARINGTON, A POET-TURNED-PLUMBER...

YE DO A POO, AND THEN YE FLUSH, AND BANISH IT WITH WATER'S RUSH...

IN 1596, HE BUILT HER A WOODEN LOO WITH A WATER TANK ABOVE IT TO WASH AWAY WASTES...

TANK
SEAT
HIS DESIGN

FRANKLY, WITH THIS INVENTION ALL OUR FUN WENT DOWN THE PAN — FOREVER!

WE GOT A BUM DEAL. GRRR!

BEFORE FLUSH TOILETS, PEOPLE USED POTS THEY KEPT IN THEIR BEDROOMS...

IS THERE A MONSTER UNDER THE BED?

I'D RATHER NOT SAY HOW BIG IT IS.

LOOK OUT BELOW!

THEN, IN THE MORNINGS, US POOS FLEW!

WHEEE!

FEELS LIKE RAIN...

THAT WAS A FUN WAY TO GO!

I'M SUPERPOO!

ME TOO!

THE INVENTION OF THE FLUSH TOILET MEANS WE NOW MEET A WATERY END INSTEAD...

HELP! I CAN'T SWIM!

NOR ME!

TO MAKE THINGS WORSE, BRITISH PLUMBER THOMAS CRAPPER INVENTED THE U-BEND IN THE 1860s...

FLUSH!

NOW THERE'S NO WAY BACK!

WE'RE DOOMED!

FRANKLY, US POOS HATE FLUSH TOILETS...

WE THINK THEY STINK! GRRR!

WHATEVER NEXT?
TAKE A SEAT

BOLDLY GO
The world's most expensive toilet cost over $23 million US dollars to develop. It is on board the International Space Station and uses a fan — not a flush — to suck waste inside it.

SITTING PRETTY
The most valuable loo on Earth is on display in the Hang Fung 'Hall of Gold' in Hong Kong. Solid gold, it is valued at $5 million, and no one is actually allowed to use it as a loo.

YUM OR YUK?
'Modern Toilet' is a chain of toilet-themed restaurants in Taipei, Taiwan. Customers sit on loo seats to eat food served on bathroom-style plates, including poo-shaped puddings.

IS IT ART?
The sculpture 'Fountain' by French surrealist artist Marcel Duchamp is a factory-made men's urinal laid flat and signed 'R Mutt, 1917'. Experts reckon it is the world's most important piece of modern art ever!

HIGHLY INVENTIVE
PERCY SPENCER

Hello! I'm US engineer and inventor, Percy Spencer. I wonder if my name rings a bell because my most famous invention certainly does: **the microwave oven!**

DING!

Its invention was a happy accident, though I had a less happy start myself. I had to leave school and begin work when I was just 12 years old. Later, I joined the US Navy where I taught myself all about **radiowaves** — not just ocean waves!

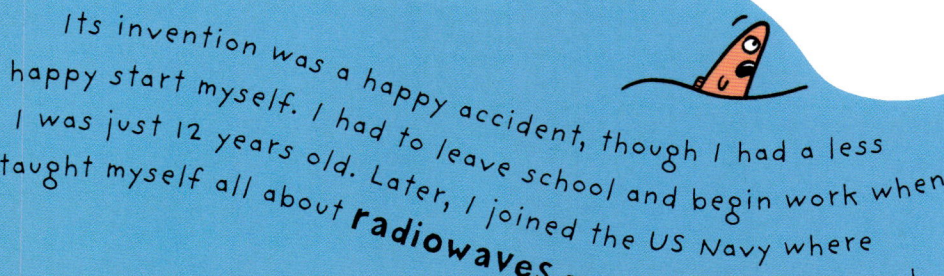

During World War Two, I worked at a big defence company developing devices called **magnetrons** that produced invisible rays called microwaves. One day, I was standing close to a magnetron when I got a warm feeling...

A chocolate bar in my pocket had melted. **DING!** I had an idea! I reckoned the invisible microwave rays were the cause of the heat. So, I tested my theory with a bag of popcorn kernels — they cooked too. **POP!**

Next, I fired microwaves at a raw egg. The invisible rays made it so hot inside that it exploded, scattering yolk over one of my colleagues. You could say we both ended up with egg on our faces. Ooops!

After all these experiments, I set about building a microwave oven people could use in their homes. Back in 1947, the first model was called the **Radarange** but — at two metres tall — it was far too big and expensive. We sold only one!

Microwaves soon got smaller though, as did the price. Nowadays, many homes have them and they are a safe and efficient way of cooking. The invisible rays heat up food by making its water molecules vibrate really fast. But now my time is up. **DING!**

BUBBLE WRAP

HI! WE'RE A PIECE OF THE POPULAR PACKING MATERIAL YOU CALL BUBBLE WRAP!
LOOK OUT! THEY'RE COMING BACK!
EEK! THE FINGERS OF DOOM!
NO! LET ME FINISH SPEAKING!
BUBBLE WRAP WAS INVENTED BACK IN 1957 BY THESE TWO GUYS, US ENGINEER ALFRED FIELDING AND SWISS CHEMIST MARC CHAVANNES...
WE HAD THIS GREAT IDEA!
IT JUST POPPED INTO OUR HEADS!
THEY GLUED TOGETHER TWO PLASTIC SHOWER CURTAINS, SEALING BUBBLES OF AIR BETWEEN THEM...
TRAPPED!
LET ME OUT!
HELP!
WHY? THEY WERE TRYING TO INVENT A NEW TYPE OF TRENDY WALLPAPER...
WHAT DO YOU THINK OF IT?
SORRY TO BURST YOUR BUBBLES, BUT NOT MUCH...
THAT FLOPPED! NEXT, THEY TRIED USING IT TO INSULATE GREENHOUSES...
IF ONLY I COULD GET CLOSER!
EEK!
ANOTHER FLOP! BACK THEN, DELICATE OBJECTS WERE SENT THROUGH THE POST PACKED WITH BALLS OF INKY NEWSPAPER.
I'VE GOT A LOT ON MY HANDS!
SADLY, IT DIDN'T ALWAYS OFFER MUCH PROTECTION...
MY SMASHING VASE SMASHED!
IN 1959, COMPUTER COMPANY IBM LAUNCHED A VERY DELICATE AND VERY EXPENSIVE NEW COMPUTER.
THE IBM 1401 WAS THE SIZE OF TWO FRIDGES!
BUBBLE WRAP TURNED OUT TO BE THE PERFECT MATERIAL TO KEEP ITS COMPUTERS SAFE DURING DELIVERY.
ANOTHER COMPUTER SAFELY DELIVERED!
AND THAT'S A WRAP!
BUBBLE WRAP WENT FROM 'FLOP' TO 'POP' WITH EVERYONE STARTING TO USE IT!
LIKE YOUR NEW VASE?
NOT AS MUCH AS THE STUFF IT WAS WRAPPED IN!
POP!
POP!
PEOPLE SAY POPPING BUBBLES HELPS RELIEVE STRESS.
NOT FOR US IT DOESN'T!
EEK!
THEY'RE BACK!

WHATEVER NEXT?
WRAP STAR

GOLDEN 'POP-PORTUNITY'
'Sealed Air', the company formed by the two inventors to produce bubble wrap, celebrated its 50th anniversary in 2010 with a limited-edition gold-coloured version.

POP ARTIST
US artist Bradley Hart copies famous paintings by injecting paint into the bubbles on giant sheets of bubble wrap.

LOVELY BUBBLY
Today, bubble wrap bubbles come in many shapes and sizes – including novelty smiley faces and love hearts!

NON-STOP POP
A 'Mugen Puchipuchi' is a Japanese electronic toy that replicates the sound and feel of bursting bubble wrap without ever running out of bubbles!

PACK IT IN!
Plastic bubble wrap can be recycled but is best kept and reused. Non-plastic alternatives include compostable packing chips made from sweetcorn and mushrooms.

39

DOMESTIC DOG

Hello, I'm here...

Down here! Come on!

That's better. I'm a dachshund. Small but with the heart of a wolf... WAG!

...a long-gone wolf that probably lived in Siberia, Russia, about 14,000 years ago.
- We ate mammoths...
- We 'wolfed' them down! Yum!

Although modern dogs are not closely related to living wolves, I'm afraid...
- Sorry!
- We're delighted!

Some scientists think our wolf ancestors hit on humans for the waste food they left around.
- They're not very tidy.
- Yes, isn't it great!
- CHOMP! CHEW!

The warmth of our fires may also have attracted them...
- I could get used to this in 14,000 years or so...

Less wary wolves may have stayed with humans...
- Good boy, Mr Waggles!
- PAT!
- Sigh! My wolf name is Bonecrusher...

Over time, dogs became the first animals to be domesticated...
- Pffh! Big deal!
- We agree...

However, us dogs reckon we domesticated you...
- Exactly!
- Yes!

Look at all the things we've got you doing for us!

FINDING FOOD | OPENING DOORS | CUDDLES | PICKING UP POO

- I'd say we are top dog here...
- What?!
- SWIPE! SCRATCH!
- Er, maybe not...

WHATEVER NEXT?
A DOG'S LIFE

ROVER'S RETURN
The retractable lead that lets a pooch pull ahead then be brought back was invented in 1908 by New Yorker, Mary A Delaney. She wanted to stop dogs getting tangled up with lampposts. Dogs love lampposts!

BROLLY GOOD!
The see-through dog umbrella was invented in 2003 by another New York citizen, Irina Zhadan-Milligan. It prevents pets getting wet when it rains, unless, of course, your poodle pootles through a puddle.

QUACKING IDEA
'Quack' is a soft silicone-rubber muzzle invented in Japan that can turn a nippy dog into a nutty-looking duck with a funny, friendly smile.

EAR, EAR!
In 1980, US inventor James D Williams patented his Animal Ear Protectors — a device for keeping long-eared dogs from trailing their lengthy lugs in their food as they feast.

SHADES OF GLORY
US businesswoman Roni de Lullo invented 'Doggles' — doggy sunglasses — after playing in bright sun with her own dog, 'Midknight'. Not just a fashion item, they also protect against dust and sand, and can help dogs with dodgy eyesight.

41

WORLD OF WONDERS

GREAT MISTAKES

Pop! Ping! Bubble wrap and microwaves make different noises, but share the fact they began as accidental discoveries. Here are some other unintended inventions we have in our homes, including some top toys!

STICK WITH IT

US chemists trying to make a super-strong adhesive in 1968 accidentally produced a gentle, reusable glue instead. It took five years to think of using it on **sticky notes**, whose pale yellow colour comes simply from the spare paper they had to hand whilst developing the idea.

NUTTY PUTTY

Silly Putty was invented in 1943 by Scottish chemist James Wright who was trying to make a new type of rubber. Instead, he came up with a weird slime that bounced and stretched, but kept its shape when you hit it with a hammer. How nutty is that?

SAFETY FIRST

US mechanic Walter Hunt accidentally invented the **safety pin** in 1849. He bent a bit of wire into the form of a springy clip while wondering how to pay off a small debt. He sold his idea for just $400 to a company that then made millions from it. In the 1970s, safety pins were high fashion for punk music fans!

OFF THE WALL

Play-Doh™ craft clay was originally created for cleaning dirt off wallpaper in 1930s USA. Nursery school teachers found it a fun and safe modelling material, and it was relaunched as an artistic toy in lots of bright colours.

SPRING INTO ACTION

One day in 1943, US naval engineer Richard James knocked a spring off a shelf and watched as it 'walked' down some books to the floor. He made his own improved steel coils to sell in shops, and the name **Slinky** was picked from the dictionary by his wife Betty.

CHAPTER 4
FOOD AND DRINK

It is easy to take food and drink for granted as we trundle a trolley through the supermarket. Not so long ago, our ancestors only had a field for their fruit and veg, and a herd of mammoths served as a mobile meat counter. In many ways, we really do have life today on a plate. In this chapter, we chew over the stories behind our favourite things to eat and drink.

WORLD'S MOST IMPORTANT FOOD

A staple food is one lots of people rely on. Maize or corn is the world's **number one**, and the Mayan people of ancient Mexico worshipped it as a god. Show your cornflakes some respect!

WORLD'S OLDEST EDIBLE FOOD

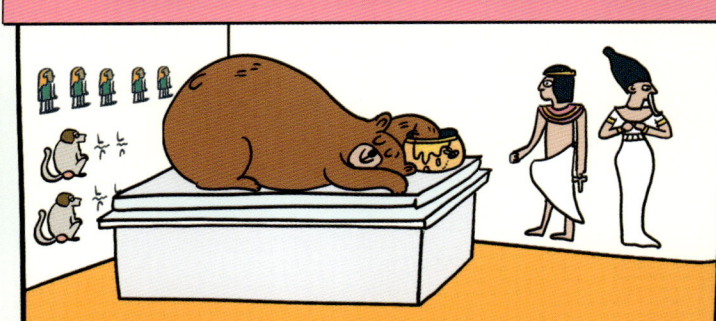

Clay jars of **5,500-year-old** honey were dug up in the country of Georgia. Honey jars were also found in the tomb of Egyptian pharaoh Tutankhamun. Do they have best-before dates?

WORLD'S HEAVIEST TURNIP

Fact meets folktale! In February 2021, Canadian Damien Allard grew an enormous turnip that weighed a whopping **29 kilograms**! Luckily, he didn't need a mouse to help him harvest it.

WORLD'S STINKIEST FRUIT

The **durian** is a prized, spiky Asian fruit that tastes delicious, but smells atrocious. In fact, its honk is so horrible that Singapore has banned it from buses and trains.

43

HAMBURGER

Hi! I am a 'meal of mystery'... ?

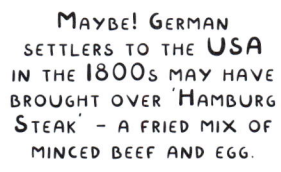

We thought you were a hamburger... Shh! Don't spoil this!

I have many names and forms...
'HAMBURGER' · 'BEEFBURGER' · 'BURGER' · 'CHEESEBURGER'

But who invented me, and is there any connection with the port of Hamburg in Germany?
- Sesame seed bun
- Lettuce
- Sauce
- Beef patty
- Gherkin

I stack-up, but do the clues?

Maybe! German settlers to the USA in the 1800s may have brought over 'Hamburg Steak' – a fried mix of minced beef and egg.
Don't I sound tasty?

This was served on a plate not in a bun.
Food's too slow this way...
I agree!

So, who first put this beef into bread?
Aha!

That's another mystery.
Ooh!

Several American chefs claim to have built the first burger...
- Me, Fletcher 'Old Dave' Davis in 1880!
- Me, 15-year-old 'Hamburger Charlie' Nagreen in 1885!
- Me, Louis 'No Nickname' Lassen in 1900!
- Us, Frank and Charles Menches in 1904!

No one knows, but it wasn't this clown.
Bah!

We do know that burgers were big news at the World's Fair in St Louis, Missouri, in 1904...

ST. LOUIS NEWS
BEEF-FILLED BUN IS FAST FOOD FUN

...and the first burger bar chain, White Castle, opened in Wichita, Kansas in 1921...
It looks like a castle!
Maybe a Burger King lives there!

So, if you're just a filling between some bread, why aren't you called a 'sandwich'?
Hmm... another mystery...

WHATEVER NEXT?
HAND TO MOUTH

FULL OF BEANS

The meatless veggie burger was invented in 1982 by chef Gregory Sams. Not having eaten meat since he was a child, getting it to taste right took him quite some time!

BIT OF A MOUTHFUL

The double-decker Big Mac burger sold by the McDonald's fast food chain was invented in the USA in 1967. It was called 'The Aristocrat', but customers weren't sure how to pronounce its name so it was soon changed.

HOT STUFF

In India, where eating beef is unpopular, McDonald's sells a chicken-based substitute called the Maharaja Mac. There is also a spicy meat-free Tikki Burger made with potatoes and peas.

RED ALERT

Wendy's burger chain was named after the eight-year-old daughter of the company's founder, Dave Thomas. Her name was actually Melinda, but she was known at home as Wendy — and is the copper-haired girl in the company logo.

MEALS ON WHEELS

The world's smallest working burger van was built by British inventor Yannick Read for his three children, Olive, Bertie and Noah. At just 1.6 metres long, they can cook up suitably small burgers just a quarter of the normal size.

HUNGRY FOR KNOWLEDGE

McDonald's runs a number of Hamburger Universities around the world where you can study for a degree in 'hamburgerology'!

FIZZY DRINKS

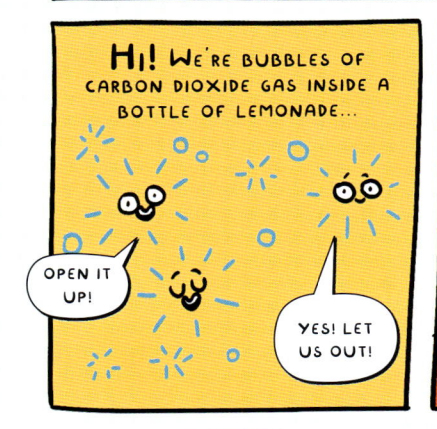

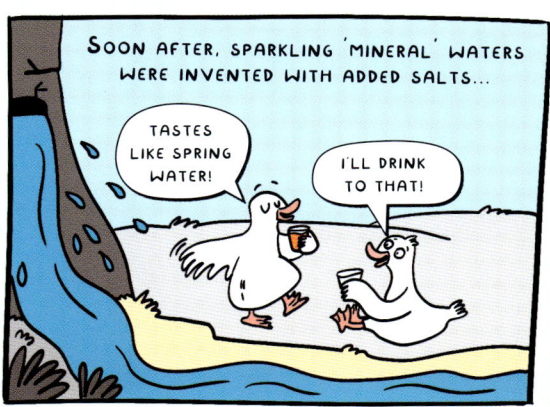

Hi! We're bubbles of carbon dioxide gas inside a bottle of lemonade...
- Open it up!
- Yes! Let us out!

We're what makes pop 'pop' when it is poured!
- That's better!
- POP!
- FIZZ!
- Thanks!

Sparkling soft drinks were invented by English chemist Joseph Priestley in 1767...
- I dissolved carbon dioxide gas in water...
- He's the whizz who made fizz!

Swiss scientist Johann Jacob Schweppe took his idea and made the first soda water in London in 1792...
- The name came from the chemical I used to make my bubbles.

Soon after, sparkling 'mineral' waters were invented with added salts...
- Tastes like spring water!
- I'll drink to that!

The big breakthrough was adding sugar and flavours like lemon and ginger...
- Life is sweet!
- I'll drink to that too!

Early soft drinks were sold at chemist shops as health tonics...
- Take two glasses three times a day.
- You bet! Yum!

Special bottles were needed 150 years ago to keep in the fizz.
- My shape kept the cork wet!
- I used a marble stopper!

Then, in 1892, crown-shaped metal caps were invented...
- I declare this bottle open!

Aluminium cans came along in 1957...
- I can be recycled forever!

ROYAL CROWN COLA, USA

And plastic bottles have been around since the 1970s...
- We are lighter than glass...
- Big deal!

But, sadly, many of them still are - with lots in our oceans...

So, remember to recycle them!
- FIZZ!
- BYE!
- POP!

WHATEVER NEXT?
TOP OF THE POPS

THE FIRST STRAW
Drinking straws were originally just a dried, hollow grass stem through which a drink was sipped. American Marvin C Stone invented the rolled paper version in 1888 as he hated the taste the grassy straw added.

BEAT THAT BOTTLE!
The curvy Coca-Cola bottle was created in 1915 to make the drink stand out from its rivals, and so it could be recognised by touch alone. The world's largest Coke bottle stands outside a mall in Las Vegas, Nevada, USA, and is 30 metres tall!

BEND IT LIKE FRIEDMAN
Bendy straws were invented by another American, Joseph B Friedman, in 1937. He came up with the idea of the flexible joint after watching his young daughter Judith struggling to use a straight straw whilst sat at a counter.

THINK BEFORE YOU THROW
Plastic bottles placed in the bin get burned or buried in the ground. However, recycled bottles can be turned back into new bottles or used to make clothing. It takes just ten to make a T-shirt and helps save the planet!

LOTS OF BOTTLE
In 2014, Czech friends Jakub Bures and Jan Kara built a boat from 50,000 fizzy drinks bottles and successfully sailed it 850 kilometres down the River Elbe to highlight the problem of plastic pollution.

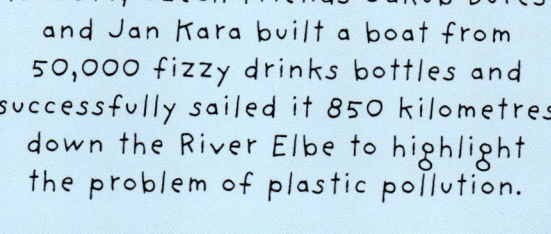

47

HIGHLY INVENTIVE MOMOFUKU ANDO

Hi! I'm Japanese businessman Momofuku Ando. Back in 1958, I invented the world's fastest fast food: **instant noodles**. You could say they were an 'instant' hit!

For many years after World War Two, food was scarce in Japan. Those with time and money would queue for hours for a bowlful of a savoury soup containing noodles made from wheat and eggs called a ramen. Was there a speedier solution?

Well, it took me many months to come up with one. I worked every day in a little wooden shed behind my house, making my own noodles and seeing if I could find a way to get them to cook more quickly. But how?

My wife **Masako** showed me the way. One day I watched her deep frying tempura batter in hot oil to produce crunchy, tasty treats. She guided me as to what to do: dry my noodles by pre-cooking them in hot oil!

Frying opened up holes in the noodles that allowed boiling water in to soften and cook them quicker. I added savoury flavourings to packs of dried noodles and, in August 1958, launched my first instant noodle snack: **chicken ramen** (my favourite!)

People loved them, and my new food business boomed! Then, in 1971, I hit on the idea of selling them in sealed pots with several flavours. Just add boiling water, stir, wait three minutes and eat! **Cup noodle was born!**

Now, about **100 billion** noodle pots are eaten each day and, in 2005, a special space version was enjoyed by a Japanese astronaut on the space shuttle. Some Japanese people say my noodle snack is an even better invention than the bullet train. Well, it's certainly just as fast!

POTATO CHIPS

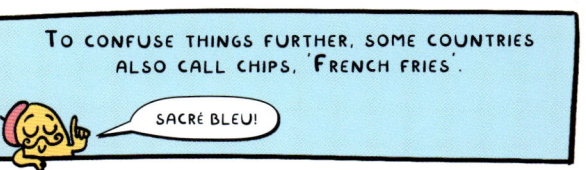

Hi! We're a pair of potato crisps!
What? It says 'Potato Chips' up there!

Well, we are certainly deep-fried super-thin slices of potato...
Nice! *SIZZLE!* *Warm in here.*

Some countries call us crisps, most call us chips.
- CHIPS
- CRISPS
- FISH

To confuse things further, some countries also call chips, 'French fries'.
Sacré bleu!

Our oldest recipe goes back to English chef William Kitchiner in 1817...
I called them 'potato shavings'... *More names!*

We became a super-snack in the 1850s when Native American chef George Speck served us at his restaurant in New York State.
My, these chips are crisp! *Thank you!* *What? Grr!*

Though some say it was actually his sister Katie Wicks who created them...
And one of them is me!

Shops soon sold them from big barrels, but the bottom chips were horrid!
Soggy! *Sorry!*

In the 1920s, US businesswoman Laura Scudder had an idea...
Keep 'em crunchy in sealed bags!

Laura claimed her crisps were the noisiest in the world...
Stop that racket! *CRUNCH! CRUNCH!* *Sorry, can't hear you!*

Flavoured chips were invented in Ireland in 1954...
Cheese and onion! *Salt and vinegar!*

Now there are over 1,000 flavours, including hot dog, lobster and chocolate.
What are we?

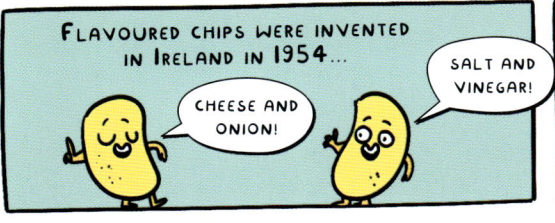

We thought of them first!

Sprout flavour! *Yuck!*

WHATEVER NEXT?
CRUNCH TIME

WHAT A GAS!
Call them 'chips' or 'crisps', snack packets are now filled with safe, inert nitrogen gas rather than just air to keep the contents crunchier!

SNACK-TASTIC!
The world's biggest bag was filled by a British crisp company in 2013. Taller than a two-storey house, it contained the equivalent of over 40,000 standard single packets.

CHIP SHAPE
Some chips come out odd-looking and can end up being auctioned online. A heart-shaped chip sold for over £250!

BAGS OF TASTE
'Ready Salted' is the world's favourite flavour. Cucumber and seaweed are popular flavours in China and Japan.

SOUND OF SILENCE
Scientists say that part of the pleasure of eating chips comes from their crunch. People who eat wearing headphones quit snacking sooner.

51

WORLD OF WONDERS

FOOD FOR THOUGHT

Some foods are named after their inventors or in honour of famous people. Imagine how sweet that would be!

WELL BREAD

Sandwiches are named after an old English aristocrat, John Montagu, the fourth **Earl of Sandwich** (a town in south-east England). The earl had his servant bring him meat between two slices of bread to eat whilst playing cards so he could carry on with his game.

ICE WORK

In 1905, American schoolboy Frank Epperson accidentally left a fruit-flavoured drink outside on a freezing night with a stirrer still in it. Upside down, it made a fabulous 'frozen drink on a stick'. Years later, his own children called it **'Pop's icicle'** – which was then shortened to 'Popsicle'.

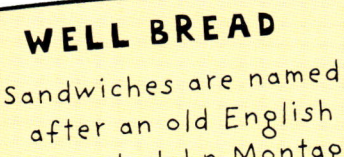

MEGA-BITE

Apple Macintosh computers are actually named after an **apple**! Jef Raskin, who worked for the newly formed company back in 1979, named their first model after the Canadian McIntosh apple, his favourite fruity food.

SLICE OF LIFE

Legend has it that Pizza Margherita was named after **Queen Margherita** of Savoy, who visited the city of Naples, Italy, in 1889. Naples is the birthplace of pizza, and the red tomatoes, white mozzarella cheese and green basil represent the Italian flag.

MUCHAS GRACIAS!

The Mexican dish nachos is named after its inventor Ignacio **'Nacho'** Anaya. In 1940, he melted cheese over a pile of tortilla chips and chilli peppers to create a speedy snack for customers at a club close to the US border.

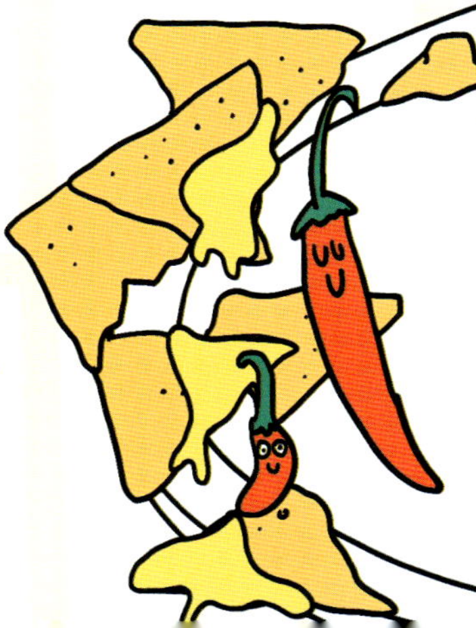

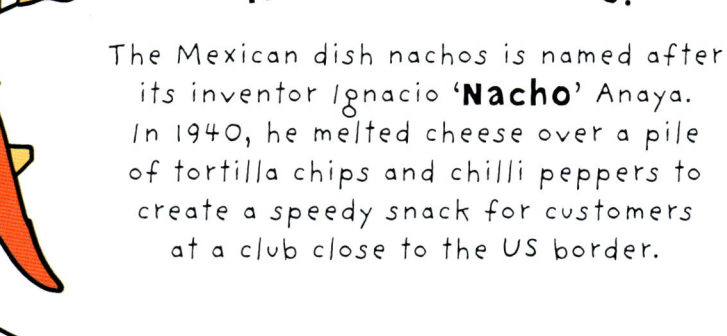

CHAPTER 5
WEAR AND TEAR

Humans have been waking up each morning and wondering what to wear for tens of thousands of years. Our first clothes came from furs, leather and tree bark. Today we use synthetic materials like nylon and plastics to make cheap clothing that we often chuck away when fashions change. In this chapter, we look at some items of everyday armour we have in our wardrobes. Here are some wearable bits of history:

WORLD'S OLDEST SOCKS

SOCKS WITH SANDALS... REALLY?

Knitted from bright red wool, these socks date back to Egypt, about **1,700 years** ago. They had lobster-like toes so they could be worn with sandals.

YOUR FIRST FASHION ITEM

For most of us, this was a **disposable nappy**! US inventor Marion Donovan hit on the idea back in the 1940s. Today, reusable cloth versions are far more eco-friendly.

MOST FIREPROOF FABRIC

Kevlar, a super-tough material that resists heat and tearing, was created by US chemist Stephanie Kwolek in 1965. Firefighters wearing her Kevlar clothing can walk through flames!

MOST EXPENSIVE SUIT

I NEED TO BOLDLY GO...

US space agency NASA is developing a new spacesuit that costs about **$500 million**! Even at this price, wearers need a giant nappy called a Maximum Absorbency Garment (MAG) to use the loo outside!

DENIM JEANS

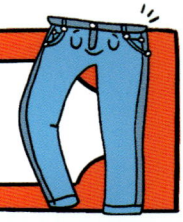

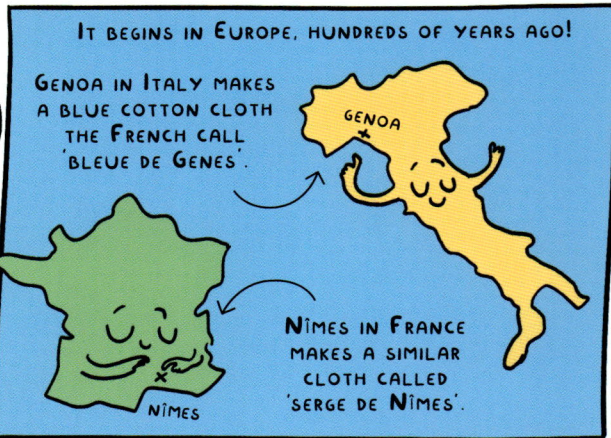

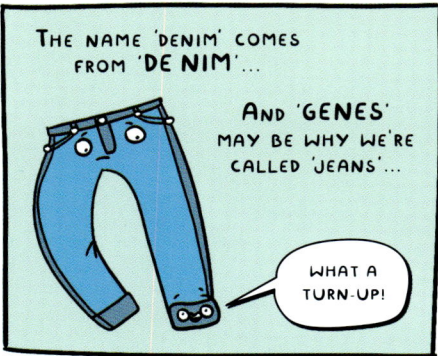

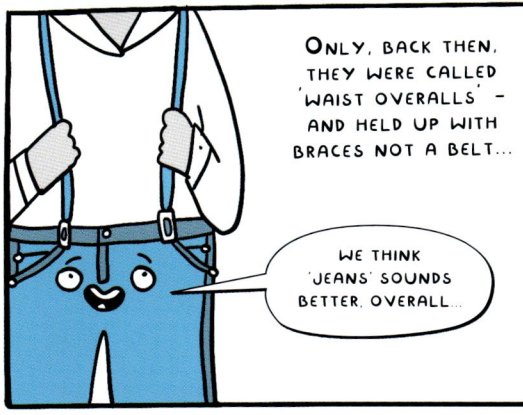

Hi! We're a pair of blue jeans! Let us tell you a story!

This story has legs — and it's riveting too! That's right! Yay!

It begins in Europe, hundreds of years ago! Genoa in Italy makes a blue cotton cloth the French call 'bleue de Genes'. Nîmes in France makes a similar cloth called 'serge de Nîmes'.

The name 'denim' comes from 'DE NIM'... And 'GENES' may be why we're called 'JEANS'... What a turn-up!

Now, let's leap to Reno, Nevada, USA, in 1871 and tailor Jacob W Davis... I sew rough, tough stuff for wild west working people!

One day he makes the pocket-seams of a pair of work trousers super-strong using copper rivets. We said this story was 'riveting'!

These power-pocket pants soon catch on — especially in blue denim. I'm trousering lots of 'pocket' money from making them!

He buys his denim from a dealer called Levi Strauss... Recognise the name?!

Between them, they hatch a plan... We need to protect our pants! Copy that — or, rather, don't!

So, in 1873, they obtain a legal patent to stop people copying their idea. Blue jeans are born! US PATENT NO. 139,121

Only, back then, they were called 'waist overalls' — and held up with braces not a belt... We think 'jeans' sounds better, overall...

Their patented pants took off — and jeans are now worn worldwide. You've all got the blues... But in a good way! Bye!

WHATEVER NEXT? JEAN SCENE

CREASE ME UP
The light creases that form in jeans with wear have special names. 'Whiskers' fan out at the front, criss-cross 'honeycomb' creases form behind the knees, and 'stacks' are faded lines above the ankle. They all make vintage jeans more valuable!

JEAN'S JEANS?
Lady Levi's were the first denim jeans made especially for females in 1934. They were intended as workwear, but were also popular with women who went on Wild West holidays inspired by Hollywood films.

BLUE PLANET
Making jeans uses lots of water — including growing cotton, dyeing the denim, and stonewashing to distress it. Make your wardrobe more eco-friendly by patching rips and owning them for longer.

WHAT A GOLDMINE
The oldest surviving pair of Levi jeans dates back to 1879 and were found in a former gold mine. They are so valuable they are kept in a fireproof safe that only two people can open.

ZIP CODE
Many modern jeans have a zip with the letters YKK on the slider. These are the initials of the Yoshida Kogyo Kabushikikaisha company of Tokyo, Japan, which supplies most of the world's zip fasteners. Now you know!

SAVE THE PLANET

55

SPORTS SHOE

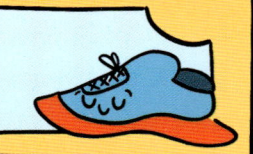

Hi! We're a pair of hi-tech sports shoes!

Join us for a jog through history!

The world's first sports shoes were created in the USA in 1868...

← CANVAS UPPER

RUBBER SOLE ↗

They were made for the ball game croquet.

Cool shoes!

I went through hoops to get them!

Similar shoes were worn for tennis – their silent soles winning them a nickname...

They're calling us 'sneakers'...

How rude!

In 1917, Marquis Mills Converse launched his now-famous All Stars basketball shoes...

They're a longshot.

My favourite sort.

Adolf 'Adi' Dassler started another big brand in Germany in 1924...

Hmm, I wonder what to call it?

Did you guess? 'Adidas' sports shoes helped legendary African-American athlete Jesse Owens win big at the 1936 Olympics in Berlin!

They were worth their weight in golds...

Adidas became huge. Then, in 1964, Americans Phil Knight and Bill Bowerman started a new track-shoe company...

Blue Ribbon Sports.

Not heard of it?

Renamed Nike in 1970, after the ancient Greek goddess of victory, its shoes included some revolutionary designs...

NIKE CORTEZ (1972)　　NIKE MOON SHOE (1974)　　NIKE AIR MAX (1987)

There is one thing they haven't improved though...

Sorry about the pong...　*WHIFF!*

WHATEVER NEXT?
PUT A SOCK IN IT

DO YOU HAVE IT IN A SMALLER SIZE?
The world's largest trainer was displayed inside a shopping mall in Hong Kong, China, and at 6.4 metres long, it might well have fitted the Statue of Liberty.

BIG TICK
Nike's trademark 'Swoosh' was designed in 1971 by college student Carolyn Davidson. She was paid just $35, though years later the company also gave her with a swoosh-shaped diamond ring.

NET PROFIT
How much do you think your old trainers are worth? A pair of used Nike Air Ships sneakers sold for almost $1.5 million in 2021, a record price. The shoes had been worn and signed by basketball legend Michael Jordan in 1984.

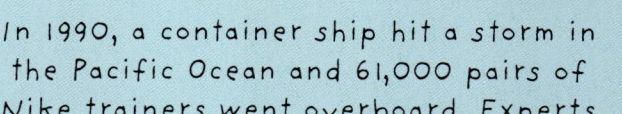

GET MY DRIFT?
In 1990, a container ship hit a storm in the Pacific Ocean and 61,000 pairs of Nike trainers went overboard. Experts used the shoes' movements to study ocean currents.

GREEN SHOES
Sports shoes and sneakers can take 1,000 years to rot away when sent to landfill. Any good, clean shoes you have outgrown are best offered to others or given to a clothing charity.

BODY AND SOLE
Japanese sports brand Asics takes its name from the first letters of the words in a 2,000-year-old phrase in Latin, the language of the ancient Romans: 'Anima sana in corpore sano' – which means 'a healthy mind in a healthy body'.

HIGHLY INVENTIVE PATSY O'CONNELL SHERMAN

Hi! I'm US chemist Patsy O'Connell Sherman. I was a woman working in science in the 1950s when sadly there weren't many of us around. Despite this, I still cleaned up with a clever invention — even if it was an accident!

"THAT'S UNUSUAL. WHAT IS IT?"

"A FEMALE SCIENTIST?"

In 1953, I was working for a big chemical company, trying to make a new type of rubber. I was in the laboratory with fellow scientist Sam Sherman, when our assistant sloshed a flask of a solution we had made and spilled some on her new white canvas shoes.

Me and Sam scrubbed and rubbed to try to remove it, but nothing worked. Soap, water, special cleaning fluids — it resisted them all. In fact, you could say we were in a **'spot' of bother!**

But here's the strange thing. That splash dried, and our assistant carried on wearing those shoes. Over time they got grubby — except where the splashed had landed. **This started us thinking...**

HMMMM...

That spot resisted dirt! We tried staining it with ink and coffee, but it stayed white! This was when we realised we had invented a fabric protector — a chemical that kept clothes from getting wet and dirty.

After lots of tests (which I couldn't attend, being a woman, grrr!) our company marketed the product worldwide. They gave it the name Scotchgard, and it's used to keep carpets, clothes and furniture safe from dirt — including the grubby paws of pets and kids!

I was lucky with my invention, but not so lucky with how I was treated back then for being a woman. That's why I went on to fight for our rights, and always said: **'Girls should follow their dreams'.**

GIRLS CAN DO ANYTHING ANYONE ELSE CAN!

59

WORLD OF WONDERS

SCHOOL RULES!

School clothes are a big part of growing up. Not all schools insist on a uniform, and they vary widely around the world. Look and learn!

BUTTON UP
School children in Italy may wear a **grembiulino** — a long apron with buttons in the front for boys and at the back for girls.

NEW SHOES, PLEASE
Japanese children change their shoes once they get to school, swapping them for **uwabaki** — soft slippers, sometimes with a coloured stripe to show what class they are in.

ANYONE FOR, ER, POLO?
Many pupils wear a **polo shirt**, first invented in 1926 by French tennis player René Lacoste. His nickname was 'The Crocodile', which became his clothing company logo.

EXPERIMENTAL CLOTHING
Pupils in Argentinian schools look like laboratory scientists in their **long white coats**. The uniform was invented by a teacher in 1915.

STICK WITH IT
School shoes often have **hook-and-loop** straps rather than laces. The fastener was invented by Swiss engineer George de Mestral in 1941 after he noticed prickly plant seeds sticking to his dog.

OLD SCHOOL
Christ's Hospital school in Sussex, UK, dates back to **1552** — as does its uniform. Pupils wear long, blue coats and knee breeches with bright yellow socks!

CHAPTER 6
FUN AND GAMES

Play is an important part of life for many animals, not just us humans. Cats and dogs, our closest companions, keep it up as adults, as do most people — even teachers! Over the centuries, humans have invented lots of weird and wonderful ways of wasting time whilst having a laugh. In this chapter, fun and games are guaranteed. Here are some top toy stories to get play underway...

OLDEST KNOWN DOLL

In 2017, archaeologists found a carved stone doll's head in a remote region of Siberia, Russia, that may be **4,500 years old**. However, the first human playthings were probably just sticks. Ask your dog!

BEST-SELLING DOLL

EMBARRASSING?

The **Barbie** doll was invented in 1959 by US businesswoman Ruth Handler. Barbie was named after Ruth's daughter Barbara, and Barbie's boyfriend Ken (since 1961) was named after her son, Kenneth.

WORLD'S SWEETEST DOLL

Stretch Armstrong, launched in the USA in 1976, can be stretched to over four times his size, and keeps his new shape (he is filled with a **thick sugary syrup**) before finally shrinking back.

WORLD'S CRAZIEST CRAZE

Cabbage Patch Kids were chubby-faced cloth dolls that the world went mad for in the 1980s. People fought each other in shops to try and buy them. Ask your parents!

61

SKATEBOARD

Yo, buds! I'm a board with a pretty sick trick... FLY!

I can flip through the air — and history too! Come with me to the early 1700s!

Back then, some unknown Dutch dude invented a wooden-wheeled device to ice-skate in summer... No ice? No problem! Hot stuff!

Then in 1759, Belgium boffin John Joseph Merlin made a mega metal version... Well, I am named Merlin. Wizard idea!

But it's totally bogus when he smashes a mirror at a party while playing a violin... Oops! Fiddlesticks!

Then in Paris, France, 1819, Charles-Louis Petibled bags the first skate patent... My design really got things rolling...

But, man, you could only sk8 str8! Come back, Monsieur! I can't! WHIZZ!

Luckily, US inventor James Plimpton created steerable skates in 1863. I did you all a good turn

After that, sk8s got gr8! 1900s / 1950s

In the 1950s, some surfer dudes on the West Coast, USA, stuck wheels on wood and invented the skateboard! We're sidewalk surfing... And here's a big wave! WAVE!

Today, I'm a board to be adored, dudes... Yo! Deck, Kicktail, Urethane wheel, Truck, Bearings ...still crash though. Oof!

WHATEVER NEXT? MOVE IT!

YOU GO POGO?

The modern pogo stick was invented in 1920 and named after its German inventors, Max **PO**hlig and Ernst **GO**ttschall. Today, the toy has turned into an extreme sport — Xpogo — where skateboard-style tricks are attempted and people can pogo over three metres high!

HOP TO IT!

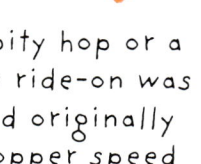

Call it a spacehopper, a hoppity hop or a kangaroo ball, the big bouncy ride-on was invented in Italy in 1968, and originally named Pon-pon. The spacehopper speed record for 100 metres is 30.2 seconds and has stood since 2004. Could you beat it?

BANGERS AND DASH

The folding micro-scooter was thought up by former Swiss banker Wim Ouboter in 1997 as a speedy way to reach a favourite Zurich sausage shop without having to use his car. Stunt scooters now do tricks worldwide alongside skateboards.

FUTURE SUCCESS

China-born Shane Chen patented the two-wheeled electric hoverboard in 2011. Though they don't actually hover, hoverboards are named after a floating skateboard in the fun sci-fi film, Back to the Future Part II, set in 2015. Shane beat them to it!

TEDDY BEAR

Hi! I'm a teddy bear. Excuse my tummy...
GRRROWLL!

Everyone loves us but who invented us?
SQUEEZE!
I LOVE YOU MR SNUGGLES!
OOF!

Well, this is German toymaker Margarete Steiff, a wheelchair user from childhood...
I sew stuffed toys and sell them... lots!

In 1902, her nephew Richard sketched bears at the local zoo...
KEEP STILL!
I hope he gets my good side...

Richard drew a pattern for a stuffed toy bear and Margarete made it up.
How is it going?
Sew far, sew good...

They called their first model 'PB55'...
Hmm, I would have preferred 'Mr Snuggles'...

Their bear was a hit at a 1903 toy fair...
I'll take 3,000 for the USA!
WUNDER-BEAR!

Meanwhile, it made news in 1902 when US President Theodore Roosevelt refused to shoot a wild bear cub...
I can't bear to do it...

This inspired New Yorker Morris Michtom to make a toy to sell in his shop...
I shall call it 'Teddy's Bear'...

'Teddy' was the President's nickname...
It was a name I hated... cute toy though...
THANK YOU!

The public went wild for Morris and Margarete's bears, and now we're probably the world's best loved toys...
Maybe some of us have been loved too much?

Nah! That's impossible! BYE!
HUG!

WHATEVER NEXT?
BEAR FACTS

BEAR WITH ME
Winnie-the-Pooh is probably the world's best-known bear. The loveable character was based on a real teddy bear — named Edward — that English author A A Milne bought for his son, Christopher Robin, in 1921.

SHELF LIFE
Paddington, the accident-prone bear from Peru, is another storybook bear based on an actual teddy. His creator Michael Bond spotted a lonely ted on a toy shop shelf on Christmas Eve, 1956, and rescued him. Early Paddington teddies were given wellington boots so they would stand-up more easily.

TED TALK
The noisemaker found inside many teddies is known as a 'growler'. It was introduced into bears by the Steiff company in 1908, and is a strong cardboard cylinder with holes that produces a friendly 'growl' when you tip it back and forth.

SMALL WORLD
The world's smallest teddy with moveable, jointed arms and legs is just 4.5 millimetres tall. Tiny Ted, as he is known, was sewn by South African Cheryl Moss, who specialises in making 'microbears'. 'TT' is on display in a museum, under a magnifying glass.

GREAT BEAR
The world's largest teddy was made in Mexico in 2019 and displayed in a football stadium. It was created to celebrate Children's Day, which happens in Mexico every April 30th, with fun events in schools instead of lessons. Hooray!

HIGHLY INVENTIVE
LONNIE JOHNSON

Hi! I'm Lonnie Johnson, a US space engineer who went on to invent not one, but two of the world's top toys. You could say that all my achievements so far have been out of this world!

Back in 1982, I was working for the US space agency NASA on eco-friendly ways to keep a space probe cool on a trip to Saturn. I wanted to use water rather than the damaging gases in fridges, so I designed a special water nozzle that I tested on a tap in my bathroom at home.

SPLOOOSH!

It shot a strong stream of water across the room and into the bath. Never mind space, I thought it would make an ace **waterblaster**, so I set about building a prototype in my basement.

My first working model was made from plastic piping, a fizzy drinks bottle and other bits and pieces. I gave it to my **seven-year-old daughter Aneka** to test, and it was a hit. She soaked her friends — and they loved it!

Next came the hard part: getting my invention into the shops. It was too expensive to make and market myself, so I went into business with a toy company that launched my '**Power Drencher**' in 1990. Kids went crazy for it!

Don't recognise the name? Well, a year later it was relaunched as the '**Super Soaker**'. An even bigger toy company then took it over and today it has sold over 250 million units worldwide. Just think of all those fun water-fights!

But, hey, I didn't stop there. In 1996, I adapted my design to fire soft foam missiles using air not water, and the Nerf Blaster was born. Frankly, I'm a hot shot when it comes to creating toys, and I want to see lots more Black inventors like me! **Go for it!**

TOY BALLOON

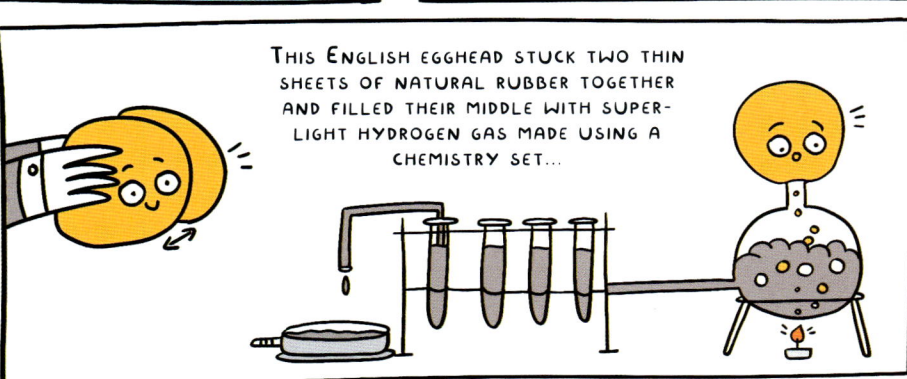

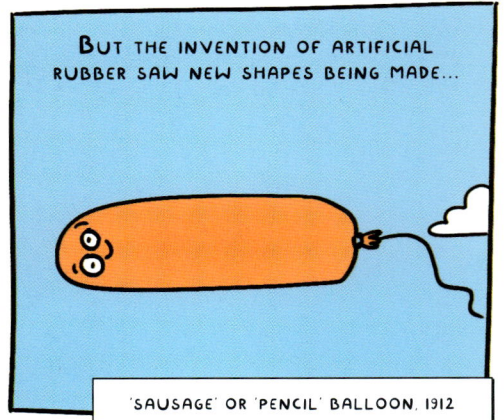

Hi! We're rubber balloons – the toys that make every party go with a bang!

SEE WHAT I MEAN?!

OOPS!

BANG!

Hard to believe, but we were invented by this man – super-serious scientist Michael Faraday in 1824!

I also invented the electric motor! See page 18

To put it another way, us balloons were first invented about 200 years ago!

This English egghead stuck two thin sheets of natural rubber together and filled their middle with super-light hydrogen gas made using a chemistry set...

Even super-serious Faraday enjoyed the sight of the gas-filled balloons.

IT GAVE ME A LIFT!

FLOAT!

The first toy balloons were round or oval, like me...

CUDDLY!

But the invention of artificial rubber saw new shapes being made...

'SAUSAGE' OR 'PENCIL' BALLOON, 1912

The USA went big on balloons – especially the novelty version invented by Neil Tillotson in 1931...

CARDBOARD EARS

HAND-PAINTED FACE

THE 'TILLYCAT BALLOON', 1931

Balloon-modelling using long, thin balloons also started around the same time...

IT'S A NEW TWIST ON TOY BALLOONS!

Amazing history for such a small thing, but now I have to fly...

WHEEE!

PRRRRRP!

WHATEVER NEXT?
BALLOON-ACY!

STICK WITH IT
Disgusting as it sounds, before rubber balloons were invented, people would blow into the bladders of dead animals such as pigs, and bounce them about. Court jesters in medieval times tied them to sticks and teased people with them.

UP AND AWAY!
In July 1982, American Larry Walters tied 45 helium balloons to a garden chair and lifted off on a 45-minute flight over California — eventually crashing into some power lines. His crazy exploits later inspired the film *Up*.

BANG ON!
The noise made by a bursting balloon is actually a tiny sonic boom — the split rubber moving close to the speed of sound!

SHRINKING FEELING
Modern toy balloons are filled with super-safe helium gas rather than potentially explosive hydrogen. Tiny helium molecules can escape through the walls of rubber balloons so plastic foil balloons are used instead — a material first developed for use in space!

WORLD OF WONDERS

PLANET MIRTH!

There's a whole world of fun to be had from playing games. Here are some popular pastimes from across the planet.

Danger game **Jenga** was created in Ghana, Africa, by Leslie Scott and launched in 1983. She took the game's name from 'kujenga', a Swahili word meaning 'to build'.

Galimoto wire cars are the ultimate recycled ride. The toys are made from scrap wire by children in many African countries and are popular tourist souvenirs.

The board game **Ludo** is based on the ancient Indian game pachisi, where players threw cowrie shells to score points instead of rolling dice.

Sophie the giraffe is a famous French toy that babies love to chew. They have been nibbling on its natural rubber neck since 1961.

Rubik's cube is probably Hungary's most infuriating invention. Created by architect Ernö Rubik in 1974, a cube can be twisted 43 quintillion different ways!

CHAPTER 7
RUN AND JUMP

Humans are highly competitive. Early sports events may well have been stone and spear throwing, like the javelin and shot put of modern athletics. The ancient Greeks gave sports a spurt, but many of our most popular games were invented less than 200 years ago. Now, grab a stopwatch and a friend: who can read this introduction out loud the fastest?

WORLD'S FIRST OLYMPIC CHAMPION

Coroebus of Elis, a cook, won the **foot-race** at the first recorded Olympic Games held in ancient Greece in 776 BCE. He was handed an olive wreath and hailed a hero.

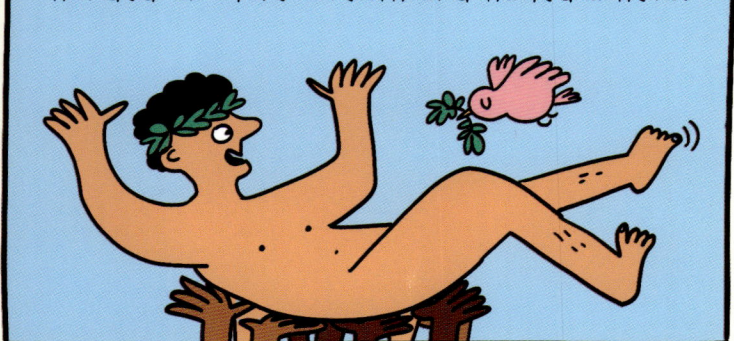

WORLD'S SECOND BEST SPORT

After football, comes **volleyball**. It was invented in the USA in 1895 as a cross between basketball and badminton, and originally called mintonette.

WORLD'S OLDEST BALL GAME

Ancient Mayans played a game using a solid ball of natural rubber on special courts over **2,000 years ago**. The ball was so heavy it probably broke bones.

NEWEST OLYMPIC SPORTS

Breakdancing, surfing and skateboarding are all new Olympic events. 13-year-old Momiji Nishiya of Japan won the women's **street skateboarding** in the 2020 summer games, making her the third youngest Olympic gold medallist.

71

FOOTBALL

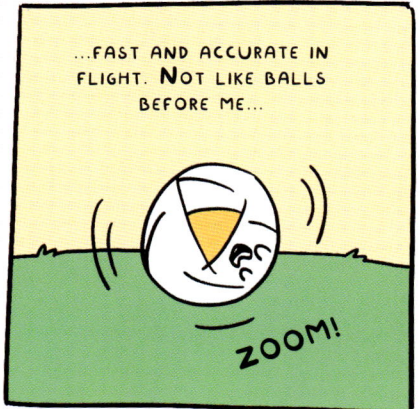

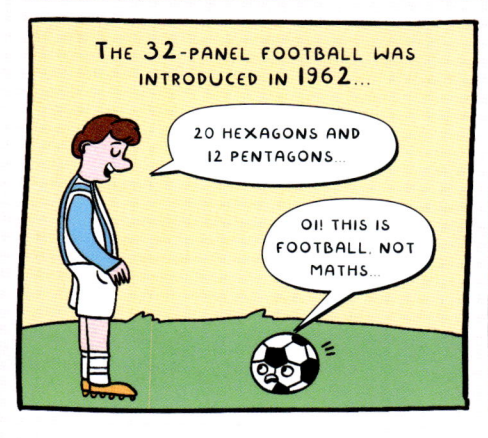

Hi! I'm a super-modern football – 20 plastic panels, eco-friendly printing, and...

...fast and accurate in flight. Not like balls before me... ZOOM!

The oldest surviving football dates from 1540, and Queen Mary the First of Scotland...
- ON ME TIARA, SON!
- OCH AYE, YOUR MAJESTY!
KICK!

For centuries, people used blown-up pigs' bladders as balls...
- I'M NOT ENJOYING THIS GAME...

Later, leather covers were added, but balls didn't always roll right...
- BAH! MY GOAL WAS TO SCORE!
- MISSED!

Luckily, US chemist Charles Goodyear invented a new type of strong rubber in 1839...
- SPORTING OF ME, EH?

Rubber bladders were used inside leather balls but went flat during matches...
- WHAT A LET DOWN...
- PFFFH!

Leather balls also soaked up rainwater making them heavy...
- OOF! THAT HURTS!
- I AGREE!

Balls changed a lot over the years...
- 1860s
- 1900s
- 1930s
- 1950s

The 32-panel football was introduced in 1962...
- 20 HEXAGONS AND 12 PENTAGONS...
- OI! THIS IS FOOTBALL, NOT MATHS...

And a ball with black patches called the Adidas Telstar was used in the 1970 World Cup Finals...
- I WAS EASY TO 'SPOT' ON TV!

Today, many hi-tech balls contain microchips so they can be tracked...

I hope they find me up here... BYE!

WHATEVER NEXT?
KICK-START

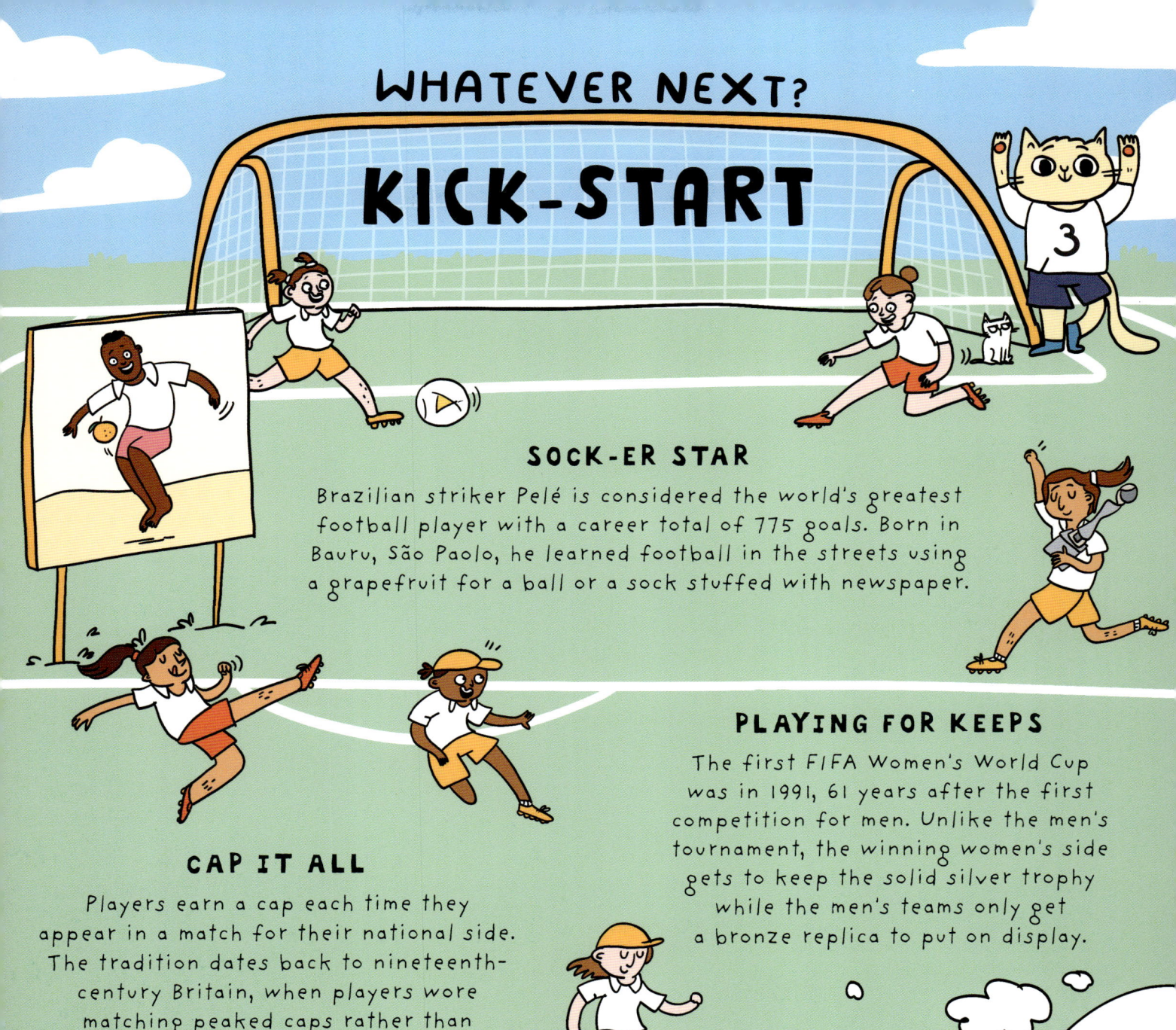

SOCK-ER STAR
Brazilian striker Pelé is considered the world's greatest football player with a career total of 775 goals. Born in Bauru, São Paolo, he learned football in the streets using a grapefruit for a ball or a sock stuffed with newspaper.

PLAYING FOR KEEPS
The first FIFA Women's World Cup was in 1991, 61 years after the first competition for men. Unlike the men's tournament, the winning women's side gets to keep the solid silver trophy while the men's teams only get a bronze replica to put on display.

CAP IT ALL
Players earn a cap each time they appear in a match for their national side. The tradition dates back to nineteenth-century Britain, when players wore matching peaked caps rather than different coloured shirts to show which team they were on.

VANISHING ACT
The disappearing spray used by referees to mark the position of a defensive wall for a free kick was invented by Brazilian football fan Heine Allemagne in 2000. The pressurised can contains water and a small amount of vegetable oil that forms a short-lived white foam. Magic!

73

TABLE TENNIS

Hi! I used to be a big noise in sport... Down here!

In fact, that noise gave the sport a name... PING! PONG!

The game came from people wanting to play tennis indoors in the 1880s... It's tennis but on a table! What could we call it?

Bats and a net replaced books in a set sold in England in 1901... PING-PONG OR GOSSIMA

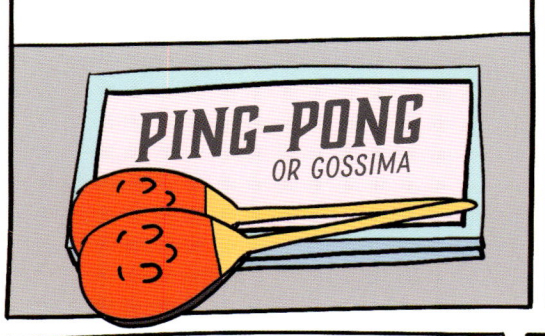

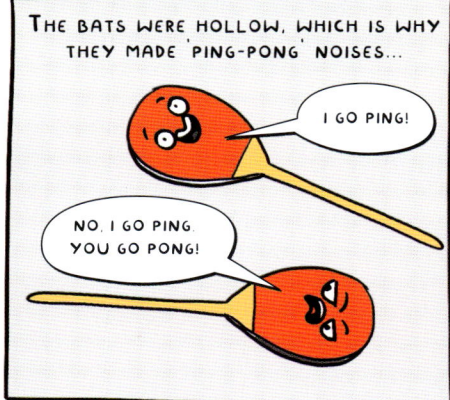

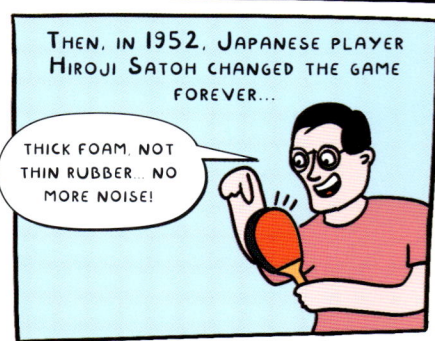

The bats were hollow, which is why they made 'ping-pong' noises... I go ping! No, I go ping, you go pong!

Ping-pong had many other names too... Who's for whiff-whaff? Pim-pam? Netto? Clip-clap, surely?

The hollow celluloid ball was invented in 1901... Not more noise! TOCK! TOCK! TOCK!

And solid wooden bats got rubber faces... You're all pimply! But we spin the ball better, old timer!

Then, in 1952, Japanese player Hiroji Satoh changed the game forever... Thick foam, not thin rubber... no more noise!

Today's bats have lots of layers to make the ball spin more and move faster... WOODEN BLADE, RUBBER, SPONGE, HANDLE

In fact, the game is now so fast, modern plastic balls got bigger to slow them down... BEFORE 2000 — 38MM — SINCE 2000 — 40MM

Me, I'm just sick of being hit all the time. Where's that ball gone? Shh! No noise!

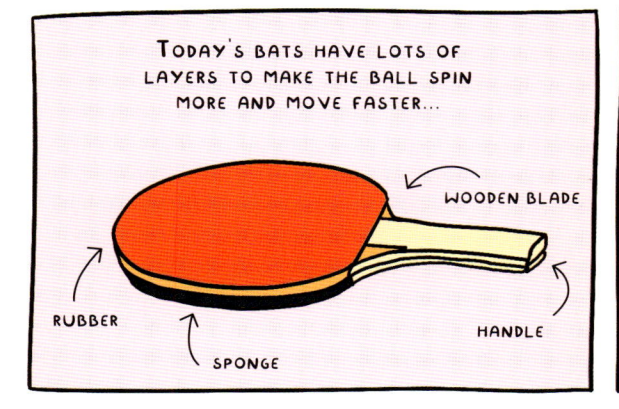

WHATEVER NEXT?
HAVING A BALL

COLOURFUL IDEA
Ball pits have been bouncing around since 1976. Their Canadian creator Eric McMillan got the idea from looking at a jar of pickled onions. The world's largest ball pit was built in China in 2015, with over two million balls!

SOFT IDEA
Soft foam balls for safe indoor play were launched in the USA in 1969. Their inventor, Reyn Guyer, originally developed the material for fake foam rocks that kids would throw at each other as part of a prehistoric caveman game. Ug! Don't hit me!

FRUIT LOOP IDEA
Basketball was invented in 1891 by Canadian PE teacher James Naismith. He nailed two closed-bottom fruit baskets to opposite ends of a gymnasium, and a ladder was needed to fetch the ball each time a slam-dunk was scored. The first basketball was actually a football.

BRIGHT IDEA
Tennis balls are made from two pieces of rubber with a stretched-8 shape. Most were once white, but it was found that 'optic yellow' balls were easier to see on colour TVs, though some insist they are lime green. Either way, dogs love 'em.

75

HIGHLY INVENTIVE KANŌ JIGORŌ

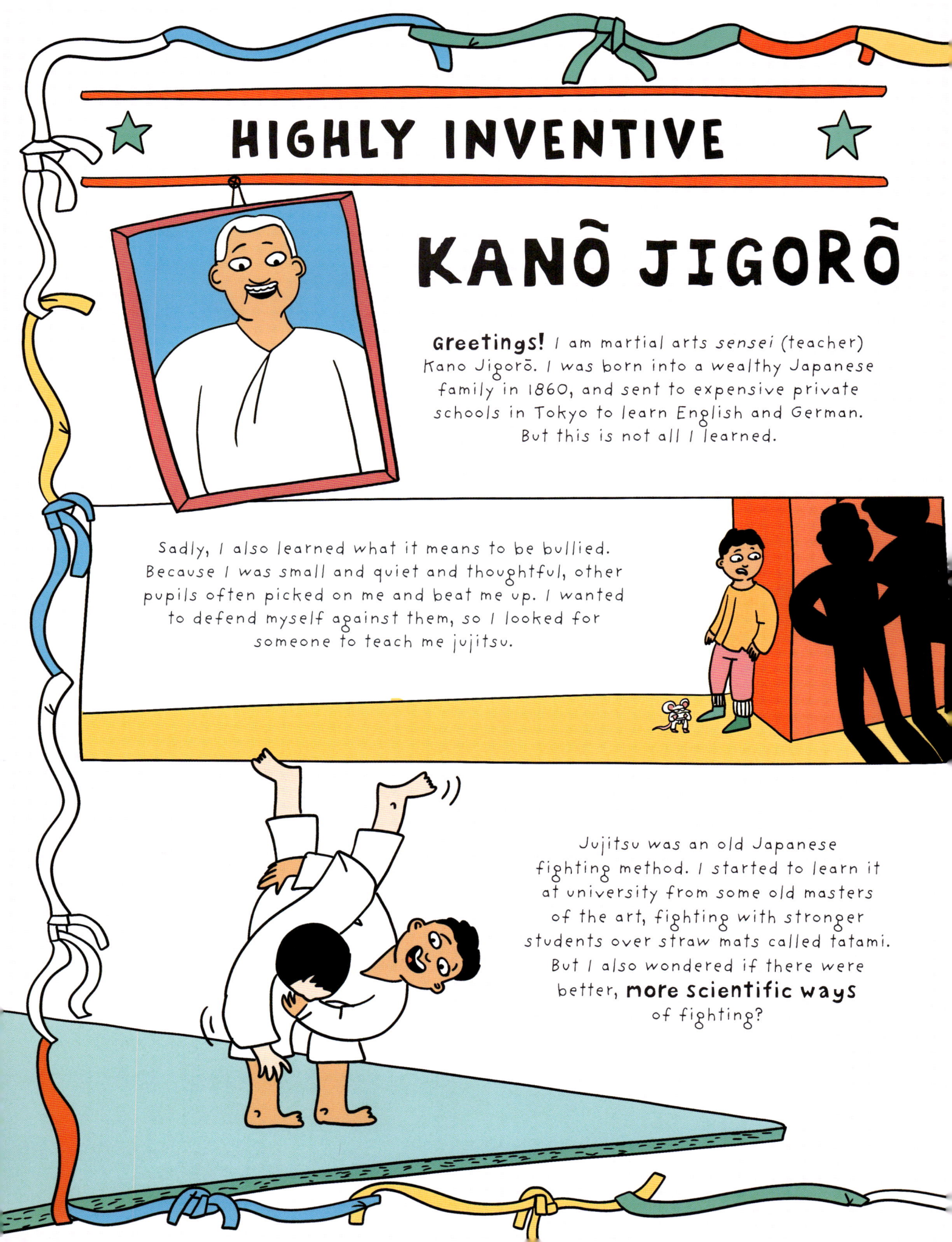

Greetings! I am martial arts *sensei* (teacher) Kano Jigorō. I was born into a wealthy Japanese family in 1860, and sent to expensive private schools in Tokyo to learn English and German. But this is not all I learned.

Sadly, I also learned what it means to be bullied. Because I was small and quiet and thoughtful, other pupils often picked on me and beat me up. I wanted to defend myself against them, so I looked for someone to teach me jujitsu.

Jujitsu was an old Japanese fighting method. I started to learn it at university from some old masters of the art, fighting with stronger students over straw mats called tatami. But I also wondered if there were better, **more scientific ways** of fighting?

One day, I used my small size to get under a much stronger and larger opponent. I wheeled him over and around my shoulders. Scientific principles of gravity, force and momentum helped me win our contest. **Result!**

Over many years, I refined my methods — taking moves from jujitsu that fitted my ideas and rejecting others.

Vitally, I realised I could beat an opponent by simply unbalancing them.

This achieved the maximum efficiency with the minimum effort.

I called my new martial art **judo**, meaning **'the gentle way'**, because it was not all about strength. I opened my own judo school or kodokan in 1884 and it soon grew from just twelve pupils to over one thousand!

Eventually judo went global, taking with it the uniform, belts, throws and philosophy I had invented. Then, in 1964, judo became the first Japanese sport to be adopted by the committee of the Olympic Games. Take that, you bullies!

77

WORLD OF WONDERS

JOLLY GOOD SPORTS!

Some of the world's most popular sports began on a small, rainy island off the coast of Europe. Football, cricket, tennis and rugby all started in the United Kingdom. Although, many other nations have their own unique sports.

Invented in Japan in 1989, **yukigassen** is an organised snowball fight. Two teams of seven start with 90 snowballs each, with a hit removing a player from the court.

Fierljeppen is a Dutch sport where competitors climb to the top of a very long pole whose other end is stuck in a muddy canal.

Gillidanda is an ancient South Asian sport. Players strike a danda — an oval piece of wood — with a long stick called a gilli, hoping it won't be caught.

Hornussen is a Swiss sport where players whack a wooden puck with large square paddles. The struck puck sounds like an angry hornet.

Bossaball was invented in Brazil in 2005. It mixes trampolines and a bouncy, inflatable court with volleyball, gymnastics and music!

Bog-snorkelling involves speeding through a peatbog in a diving mask and flippers. Oddly, it is one of the UK's less popular sports.

CHAPTER 8
SCREEN AND HEARD

Humans have been staring at screens for thousands of years. The first were probably the walls of caves, where flickering flames made drawings of bison and mammoths come alive. Then came paintings and printed pictures, before ebooks, TV screens and all our modern media. In this chapter, we get the lowdown on the hi-tech stuff that shapes our lives.

WORLD'S OLDEST COMPUTER

The Antikythera is a mysterious machine, over **2,000 years old**, that may have been an early form of computer for predicting eclipses. It was found in a shipwreck in 1901 and is still not properly understood.

FIRST TV PERSONALITY

Stooky Bill was a scarily painted dummy used by Scottish inventor John Logie Baird as a stand-in for his first experiments in television in the 1920s. Understandably, he came across as rather wooden!

MOST POPULAR CHILDREN'S E-BOOK

Electronic-reading devices have been around for decades. Started in 1971, Project Gutenberg provides classic ebooks for free. The most downloaded children's book is Lewis Carroll's **Alice's Adventures in Wonderland**.

MOST WANTED METALS

Smartphones contain many of Earth's rarest and most valuable metals including cobalt, manganese and lithium, as well as gold, silver and platinum. Hang onto devices for as long as you can and **recycle** them when you upgrade.

79

VIDEO GAMES

Panel 1: Hi! I'm a lonely homework book. Where's my owner? Well...

Panel 2: ...playing video games. Tch! WHIZZ! ZOOM! CRASH!

Panel 3: The issue goes back to US scientist Edward Condon in 1940... "My computer plays a game with matchsticks..." "Er, real matches are a lot smaller, doctor."

Panel 4: Then another US brainbox — William Higinbotham — made it worse in 1958... "The first visual computer game!" "It's a sideways look at tennis!"

Panel 5: Luckily, these were one-offs, until some students made *Spacewar!* in 1962... "We only shared it with, like, 50 people..." "Give us some space, man!"

Panel 6: Next, this guy, US inventor Ralph Baer, made things un-baer-able... "Baer with me, please!"

Panel 7: In 1972, he launched the Magnavox Odyssey, the first home video games console... HEH! HEH! "Now our conquest begins!"

Panel 8: It had a table tennis game that was copied by a rival company... BLIP! BLEEP!

Panel 9: 'Pong', as they called it, became the first arcade video game... "Me next!" "No, me!"

Panel 10: A huge hit, a home version followed in 1975... "It's like real table tennis!" "Complete with funny noises!" BLIP! BLEEP!

Panel 11: Well, US homework books have been competing with video games ever since... "What's your homework about?" "How video games began."

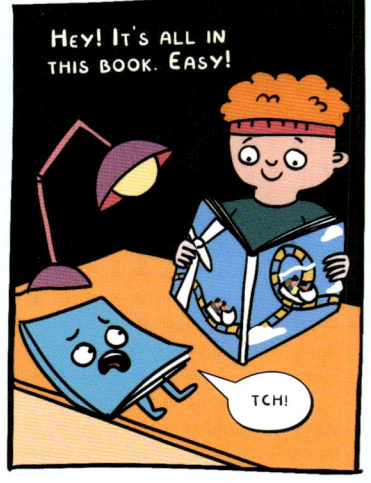

Panel 12: Hey! It's all in this book. Easy! TCH!

WHATEVER NEXT? GAME ON!

SQUID GAME
Launched in Japan in 1978, Taito's *Space Invaders* was a revolutionary arcade game. A tense 'shoot 'em up', it was the first to record player's high scores and had a musical score. Inventor Tomohiro Nishikado based the menacing aliens on crabs, squids and octopuses.

DO WEE AGREE?
The Nintendo Wii was launched in 2006, with motion-detecting remote controls allowing players to mimic sports. Some thought the word ('wee') sounded silly, but the company said the dotted 'i's were two people playing side-by-side and the 'W' was a pair of nunchuk martial arts weapons.

PLUMB CRAZY
The world's most expensive video game is an unopened copy of Nintendo's *Super Mario Bros* from 1985, which sold for a record $2 million in 2021. Plumber Mario first appeared in the 1981 game *Donkey Kong*, and was originally called *Jumpman*.

THE YOLK'S ON YOU
The first so-called 'Easter Egg' was hidden in the Atari video game *Adventure* in 1979. The game's inventor hid the words 'Created by Warren Robinett' in a secret room without telling anyone. It was only discovered after he left the company. Now 'Easter eggs' turn up in films, books and on TV as well.

TABLET COMPUTER

Hi! I'm an elephant – an animal with an amazing memory, supposedly...

Well, I can certainly remember a time before tablet computers...

Wow! And I thought my memory was big!

In fact, I can remember back to the 1940s, when computers were huge!

That's hard to process.

This ENIAC computer weighs over 27,000 kg.

Even I couldn't have carried one that size...

Puff! Strain! Help! Hand here, please...

Computers got smaller, but had only keyboards until 1968 when US inventor Douglas Engelbart created...

It looks like a mouse!

Hmm, well, it does if you do this to it...

Squeak!

The same year, US computer whizz Alan Kay had a great idea...

My KiddiComp computer for kids!

Sadly, it never got made. The world's first tablet computer was the GRidPad in 1989...

It looks great!

Early tablet computers needed a special pen called a stylus...

They're nothing to write home about...

Tablets didn't really make a mark until two big brands of 2010...

APPLE'S IPAD   SAMSUNG'S GALAXY TAB

What made them magic was touchscreen technology and a virtual keyboard...

Touch! The world is at my fingertips!

Not that elephants find it easy to use...

Ouch! Crack! Er, forget you saw that, okay?...

WHATEVER NEXT? OK COMPUTER

OH NO, THE DRAGONFLY IS DOWN!
Wireless linking system 'wi-fi' was first developed in 1990 by a US company that wanted to connect cash registers in stores. 'Wi-fi' does not actually stand for anything – it was just a catchy name that rhymed with 'hi-fi'. Earlier proposals included DragonFly or FlankSpeed.

DON'T BUG ME
A technical glitch in a computer is commonly called a 'bug'. The term is said to have been born in 1947 when US scientist Grace Hopper found a real insect inside an important computer, stopping it from working properly. The culprit was actually a small brown moth. (Sadly, dead.)

ROYAL CONNECTION
Bluetooth was invented by Swedish tech company Ericsson in 1994. It is named after the Viking king Harald Bluetooth, who lived in Scandinavia over 1,000 years ago. The Bluetooth logo combines the ancient Viking alphabet letters (runes) for the initials 'H' and 'B'.

GOLD STANDARD
The world's most expensive tablet ever is probably an iPad 2 that sold for £5 million back in 2011. The back was made from 24-carat gold with the Apple logo picked out in diamonds, while the front frame was made from a precious stone called ammolite that included a sliver of fossilised T-rex thigh bone.

HIGHLY INVENTIVE

JAWED KARIM

Hi! I'm Jawed Karim. I was born in Germany in 1979, and me, my little brother and our German mum and Bangladeshi dad all moved to Minnesota, USA, in 1992. Little did we know that was I destined to make internet history — all for just 19 seconds!

I studied computer science at college as well as working at the online payments service PayPal. That was where I met these guys, Steven Chen and Chad Hurley.

We were all frustrated by not being able to find clips of news stories and stuff like that to watch on the internet. This is when we came up with the idea to create our own video-sharing platform, YouTube.

Working out of a converted garage, Chad designed the site and the logo, and Steven and I worked on the programming. The site went live on **Valentine's Day, 2005** — but my big date was just a few weeks later, on April 23rd.

That was when we uploaded YouTube's first ever video, **'Me at the Zoo'**. It starred me and some elephants, and was shot at San Diego Zoo by a school friend, Yakov Lapitsky. It was very short but made internet history. Here's the whole thing:

UTUBE

ALL RIGHT, SO, HERE WE ARE IN FRONT OF THE, UH, ELEPHANTS, AND THE COOL THING ABOUT THESE GUYS IS THAT, IS THAT, THEY HAVE REALLY, REALLY, UM, LONG TRUNKS, AND THAT'S COOL, AND THAT'S PRETTY MUCH ALL THERE IS TO SAY.

Historic, huh? Amazingly, that first ever upload has now had over 284 million views. To me that's pretty impressive but, then again, 'Baby Shark Dance' leads the way with over 10.8 BILLION! All together now…

BABY SHARK, DUH DUH DUH DUH DUH…

SMARTPHONE

Hi! I'm a mobile phone...
— And I'm a brick.

I'm smart, and he's not...
— True.

But we do have something in common...
— We do?

Yes! In 1973, this was the first mobile phone you could buy...
— I'm the Motorola DynaTAC 8000X, and I weigh over a kilo!

Because it was so big and heavy it was nicknamed 'The Brick'!
— Like me!

Motorola guy Martin Cooper made the first public mobile call in New York City, USA, on 3 April 1973...
— Is that guy talking to a brick?

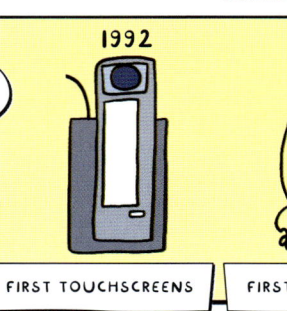

No! He called a rival phone company with a short message...
— Ha-ha! Beat you to it!

Voice calls were about all you could do with 'The Brick'...
— It's also a handy paperweight...

Mobiles took time to get smaller and smarter...

- 1992 — FIRST TOUCHSCREENS
- 1992 — FIRST TEXT MESSAGES
- 1996 — FIRST INTERNET PHONE
- 2000 — FIRST CAMERA PHONE

Then, in 2013, everyone wanted to get their hands on the new iPhone 5s...
— I'm the first with fingerprint ID!

Today, I've got all that plus wireless charging and an ultra HD camera...
— Maybe. But can you do this?

LEAP!
FALL!
— But why?
— I said I wasn't smart!
THUD!

WHATEVER NEXT?
APPY EVER AFTER

NOMNOM

Video-sharing service TikTok was developed in China in 2016. It is famed for setting some odd food trends including frozen honey, hot chocolate bombs, cloud bread and mini pancake cereal. Currently, the top TikTokker is Senegal-born Khabane 'Khaby' Lame with over 160 million followers.

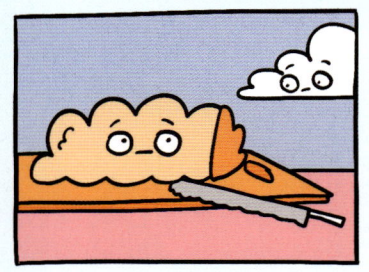

SNAP APP

Instagram started in the USA in 2010. Its name is a mix of 'instant camera' and 'telegram' — an old way of sending messages. The first photo ever posted on the site was of a seaside pier in California, with the water at a 45-degree angle. **FAIL!**

BLUE BIRD

Micro-blogging site X (formerly Twitter) was hatched in the USA in 2006. It was originally launched as twttr — no vowels — as someone already owned the web address twitter.com. The company's previous blue bird logo actually had a name — Larry — and the world-famous design only cost them $15!

SEARCH ME!

Search engine Google began from a garage in California, USA, in 1996. The name is a nod to the billions of websites the service checks for information — a 'googol' being a one followed by 100 zeroes! Incredibly popular, the word 'google', meaning to look up something online, hit the dictionaries in 2006.

PUTTING US ENCYCLOPEDIAS OUT OF A JOB!

87

BRAVE NEW WORLD

Robots doing housework. Hologram humans standing in our living rooms. All these were once the stuff of science fiction films. Now they exist for real. Some of them, like smartphones, we even take for granted. But what new marvels might the near future have in store? Strap on your jetpack, we're going in!

THE JET SET

Jetpacks already have lift-off, but flights are either rather short or rather wet. Many models work using high pressure plumes of water and so need to be flown over lakes or the ocean. Fine for the school-run if you're by the sea!

INVISIBILITY CLOAK

A wizard idea that inventors have been pottering about with for many years. The principle is simple — bring the view from behind an object to the front so it seems to disappear — but complicated in practice. Still, we may see one eventually. (Or not, if you get what we mean.)

SWEET SMELL OF SUCCESS

Scientists in Scotland have invented a clothing fabric that produces electricity from the chemicals in human sweat. The energy can be stored and used to recharge electronic devices such as smartphones and watches. No sweat!

VISION OF THE FUTURE

Bionic eyes capable of super-sight have long been part of science fiction. However, in 2021, Israeli surgeons placed an artificial sensor inside an eye that restored the vision of a man who had been blind for a decade, allowing him to see his family once more.

ARE WE NEARLY IN THE AIR YET?

Yes! Flying cars are a reality, though only as a small number of prototypes. As well as design problems, there are issues of noise, pollution and safety, as well as finding spaces for them to land and take-off. However, it is thought the cars will probably fly themselves. Enjoy the view!

THINGS TO COME

'The internet of things' is a term for the home of the future where all appliances are connected and can be controlled remotely from a smartphone. Scientists have already made a hi-tech loo that monitors your weight and health. Imagine getting a text from your toilet!

89

HIGHLY INVENTIVE YOUNG WIZARDS

Hi! I'm legendary US inventor **Thomas Alva Edison.** I had over 1,000 patents for everything from the movie camera to a reliable electric lightbulb, and despite being deaf, I also invented an early way of recording sound. The public called me 'the wizard' for the wonderful things I thought up, beginning at the age of 22. But even younger people have 'lightbulb moments' like mine. Let's meet some of these 'young wizards'.

OHIO, USA

I'm **Rifath Sharook**. In 2017, aged 18, I created the first 3D printed satellite to be shot into orbit around Earth by US space agency NASA. It weighed just 64 grams — making it the smallest and lightest satellite so far!

TAMIL NADU, INDIA

I'm **Chester Greenwood**. Back in 1873, aged just 15, I was out ice-skating when I hit on the idea of earmuffs for keeping your lugs lovely and warm. My gran helped me make my first fur-lined pair!

MAINE, USA

I'm **Louis Braille**. I was blind from the age of five but I still wanted to read. So, in 1824, I invented my own system for writing using raised dots on paper. It was named Braille, after me, and I was only 15 years old!

PARIS, FRANCE

I'm **Robert Patch**. In 1963, aged six, I patented my idea for a toy truck that could be taken apart and rebuilt in lots of different ways. I couldn't spell my name then, so I signed my design with an 'X'.

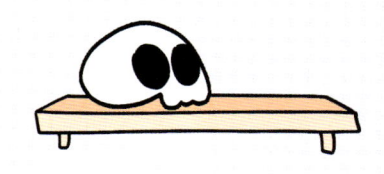

MARYLAND, USA

I'm **William Kamkwamba**. In 2001, aged just 14, I built a wind turbine to provide electricity for my family home in Wimbe village. It used parts scavenged from a scrapyard, including a bike wheel, and made me famous!

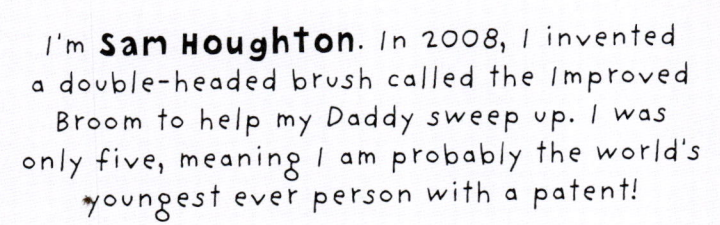

WIMBE, MALAWI

I'm **Sam Houghton**. In 2008, I invented a double-headed brush called the Improved Broom to help my Daddy sweep up. I was only five, meaning I am probably the world's youngest ever person with a patent!

DERBYSHIRE, UK

I'm **Richard Turere**. Lions attacked our family's cattle at night so, aged 11, I invented my Lion Light. I used LED bulbs from old appliances and made them flash around to look like people carrying torches. No more lions!

KITENGELA, KENYA

Hi, I'm **Macinley Butson**, and I was just six when I invented a cross between a spoon and a syringe for taking medicine. I called it the spoonge. Today, I'm a professional inventor!

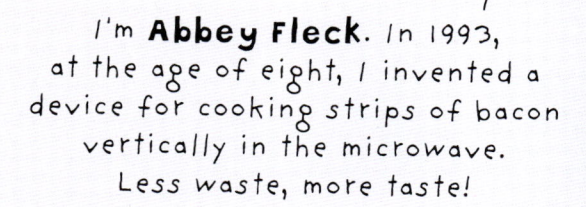

WOLLONGONG, AUSTRALIA

I'm **Abbey Fleck**. In 1993, at the age of eight, I invented a device for cooking strips of bacon vertically in the microwave. Less waste, more taste!

MINNESOTA, USA

I'm **Thato Kgatlhanye**. In 2014, I invented a schoolbag made from recycled materials with a removable solar-powered light. It helped children be seen as they walked to school in the dark, and could be used instead of a candle at home.

MOGWASE, SOUTH AFRICA

91

WHATEVER NEXT? PATENT'S PROGRESS

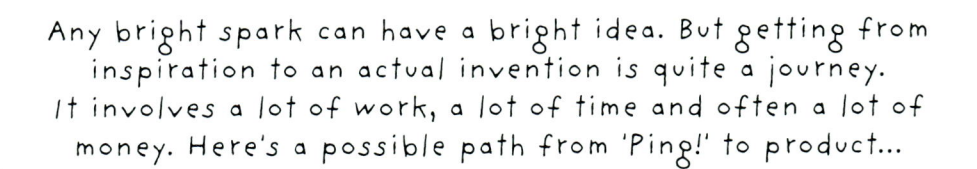

Any bright spark can have a bright idea. But getting from inspiration to an actual invention is quite a journey. It involves a lot of work, a lot of time and often a lot of money. Here's a possible path from 'Ping!' to product...

1. STRIKE IT LUCKY

PING! You are eating a banana when you are suddenly struck by a great idea: 'Fruit Loot' — points for eating fruit and veg you can swap for prizes!

2. KEEP IT QUIET

Don't tell too many people! A patent is a legal document that stops people copying your idea. You can't get one if others know about it already. Shhh!

3. CHECK IT OUT

Possibly someone else had the same idea? Search past patents and existing inventions on the internet and see if it's been done before.

5. DRAW IT UP

Sketch how your idea might look. Patent drawings don't need to be perfect but they help others get the picture.

4. WRITE IT DOWN

Grab a notebook and make dated, detailed entries about your idea. You may need to prove how and when you worked it out.

6. MAKE IT REAL
This is where it can get expensive. There are special lawyers who help inventors apply for patents, but they charge for their time — and time is money!

7. SEND IT IN
Now you must submit your idea to a national patent office. Their job is to check if it is genuinely new and useful.

8. SEND IT IN AGAIN
New ideas are often rejected first time. It is part of the process to make sure only serious ideas get patents. And it can take several years...

9. WHOOP IT UP!
Woo hoo! You've been granted a patent, meaning no one can copy your idea in your home country for the next 20 years. Now do the same worldwide.

10. MAKE IT BIG
Congratulations! Your invention is being made and sold all over the globe. Just one question remains: what will you buy with your first million?

93

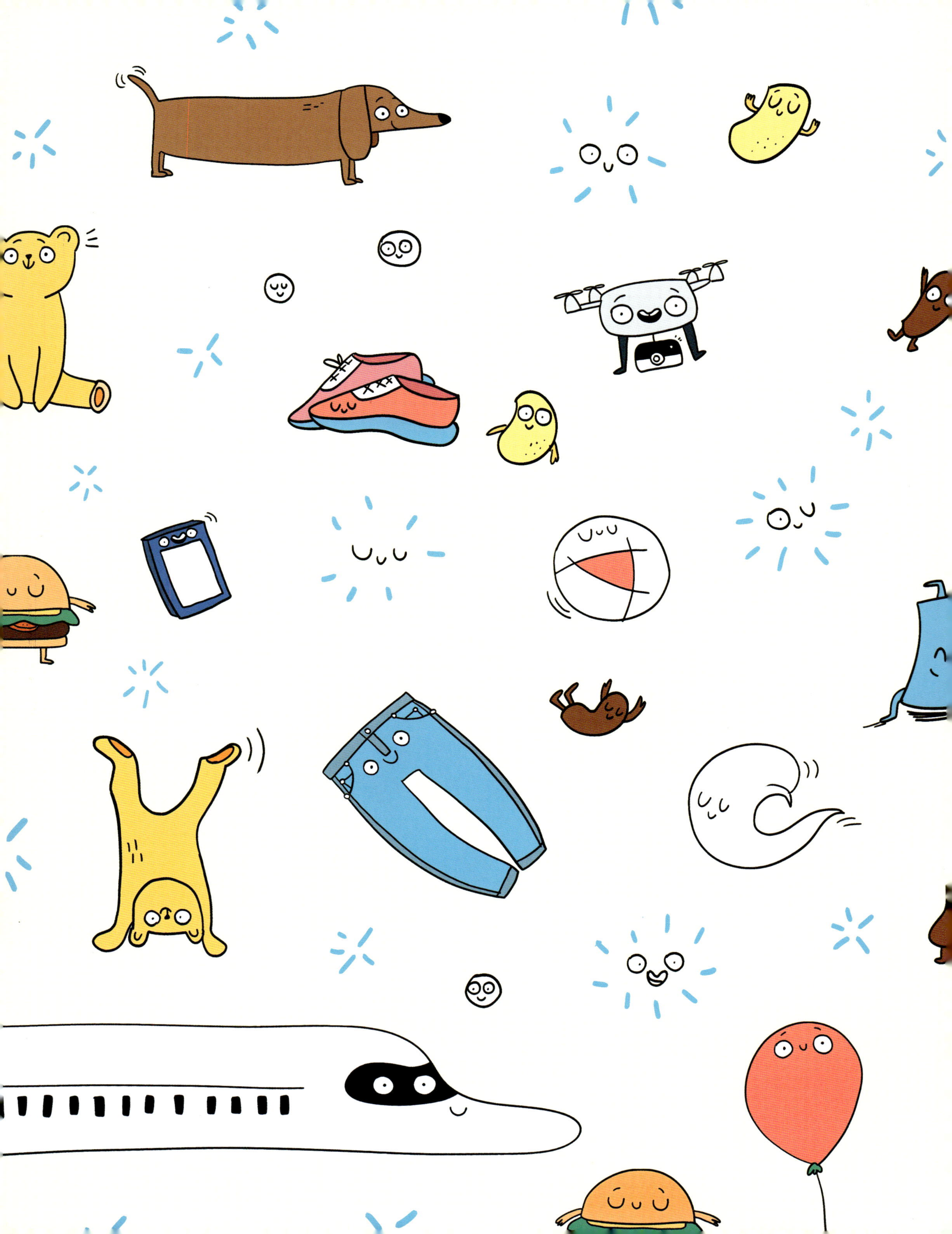

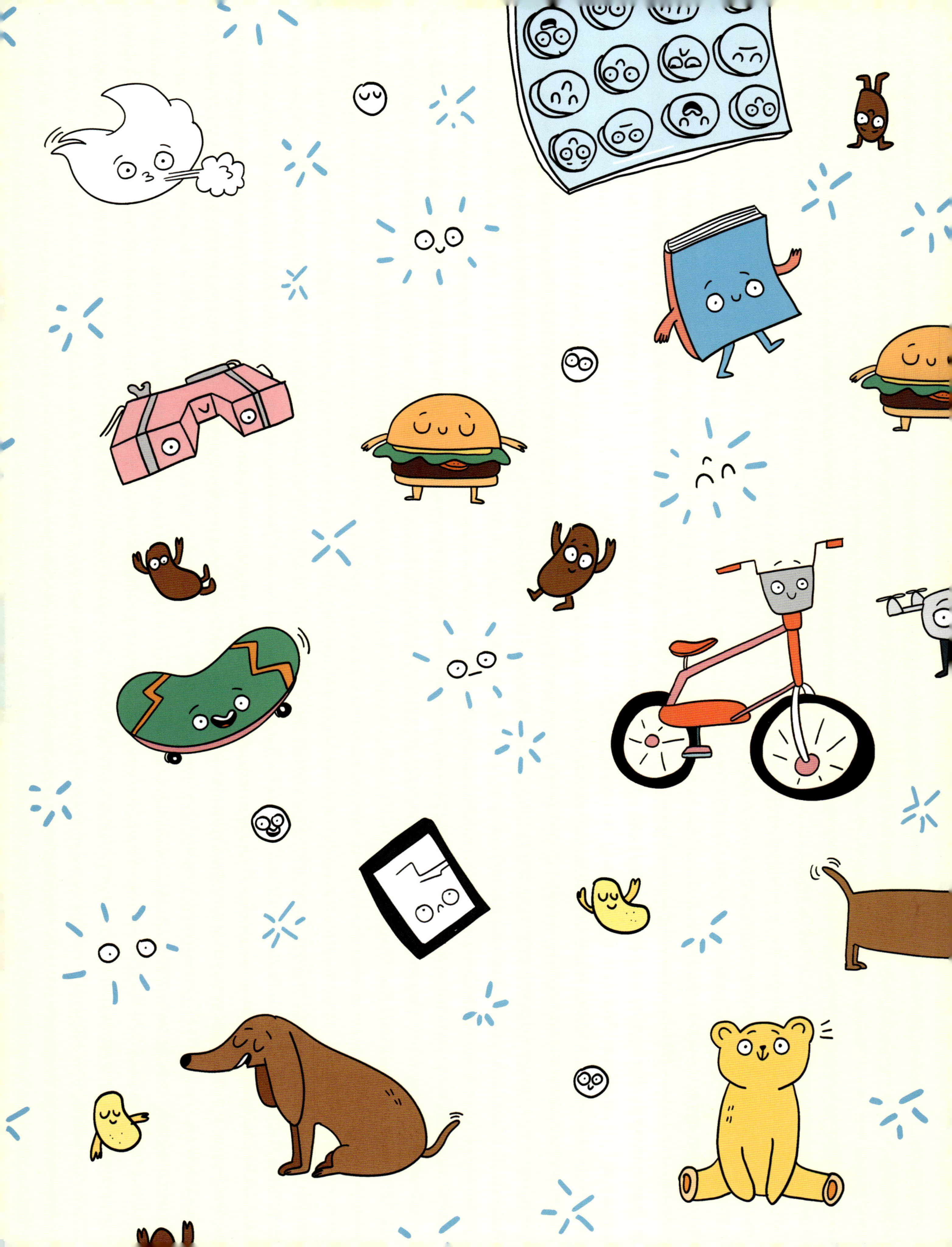

JUNIOR GENIUS

Have you got an amazing new invention?
(Copy this page and jot down your ideas – remember to keep it secret until you have a patent for it!)

DRAW YOURSELF HERE

DRAW YOUR INVENTION HERE

NAME: ....

BORN: ....

WHAT IS IT CALLED AND WHAT DOES IT DO?
....
....
....
....
....

HURRAH! YOUR INCREDIBLE INVENTION HAS MADE YOU MILLIONS! WHAT WILL YOU SPEND IT ON?
....
....
....